The writer, Alexandr Korol, was born in Saint Petersburg on the 12th of September 1990.

In 2006, Alexandr started to write his diary for the first time, where he noted his thoughts on traditional life questions: why children don't listen to their parents? Why do people lie to each other? Why don't people do what they like? As well as other thoughts about human relationships…

In 2008, Alexandr published his first book, named *Answer*, it was a compilation of author's candid thoughts from the diary. Same year, the writer adopted his mother's maiden name and since then he has written under "Alexandr Korol". His book *Answer* attracted a lot of public attention. The project became a success; Alexandr created his first YouTube video where he shared his views about the world and society. The video brought even more public interest to the writer. Video was re-posted on social networks and received more than 1 million views.

By 2018, Alexandr finished more than 10 books with a collection of thoughts from a personal diary. All of the books were available for free download on his website. The same year, the book *Corridor* was published and became a bestseller. In this book, Alexandr proposes the concept of frequency in regards to social standing and psychological state of each person. Frequency is a combination of elements of everyday life that is used by every one of us: music, movies, clothes, people around us—all of it influences the person's life. In *Corridor*, the author explains how to move from one frequency to another and which elements help or harm. In 2018, Alexandr decided to present the book to public during the event in the concert hall in Saint Petersburg, which was a wide success and attended by almost a thousand people.

Later in 2018, the second book, *Paradox,* was published. This book is a collection of separate non-fiction short stories about unexplainable events in the author's life. This diary-like book most appeals to creative and free-spirited people who believe in wonders and live by feelings. Many readers called this book a "food for the soul". The second part of this book, *Paradox 2.0,* was published in 2021. The book has the same structure and motivation to make a reader look at himself and everyday events from a different and unusual perspective.

Attention Control is a new book by the author that aims to help those who have trouble to concentrate and have problems steering their life in the right direction. The ability to control how to spend your attention is the essential part of a conscious human. This book is published in 2023.

The second book of 2023 is about women and men, friendship and friends, about relationships between parents and children and about what real love is. The author explains and gives examples of men and women's behaviour in different social strata. This book will help a reader understand themselves and other people, and build harmonious relationships with friends and loved ones.

All above books can be downloaded from the author's website: https://akinformation.com/en/

In 2022, Alexandr finished his two-part book *Have Not Charity*. This book is an exploration of relatively obscure subjects, in modern times, as sins and virtues. In 2 parts of the book, the author attempts to explain what motivates people, how life goals and peoples behaviours are affected by sins or virtues. He shows that so many "good" deeds are in fact motivated by sins. This is a modern book of ethics; the guidance for a better life. This book is an attempt to explain how society and life work. The title of the book was taken from Bible 1 Corinthians, 13-2: "and though I have all faith so that I could remove mountains, and have not charity, I am nothing."

Alexandr Korol

Have Not Charity - Volume 1: Sins and Volume 2: Virtue

Austin Macauley Publishers
LONDON * CAMBRIDGE * NEW YORK * SHARJAH

Copyright © Alexandr Korol 2023

The right of Alexandr Korol to be identified as author of this work has been asserted by the author in accordance with sections 77 and 78 of the Copyright, Designs and Patents Act 1988.

All rights reserved. No part of this publication may be reproduced, stored in a retrieval system, or transmitted in any form or by any means, electronic, mechanical, photocopying, recording, or otherwise, without the prior permission of the publishers.

Any person who commits any unauthorised act in relation to this publication may be liable to criminal prosecution and civil claims for damages.

A CIP catalogue record for this title is available from the British Library.

ISBN 9781788785983 (Paperback)
ISBN 9781788785990 (Hardback)
ISBN 9781528903981 (ePub e-book)
ISBN 9781528900881 (Audiobook)

www.austinmacauley.com

First Published 2023
Austin Macauley Publishers Ltd®
1 Canada Square
Canary Wharf
London
E14 5AA

Table of Contents

Volume One: Sins   11
   Introduction   13
   Pride   16
      Question and Answers about Pride   21
   Envy   32
      Questions and Answers about Envy   33
   Anger   49
      Questions and Answer about Anger   51
   Lust   73
      Questions and Answers about Lust   77
   Gluttony   87
      Questions and Answer about Gluttony   88
   Greed   94
      Questions and Answers about Greed   95
   Despair   113
      Questions and Answers about Despair   115
   Negative Traits   124
   The Ten Commandments   128
   Readers' Questions and Answers   131
   A Final Word   134

Volume Two: Virtues	**137**
Introduction	*139*
Prudence	*141*
Question and Answers about Prudence	142
Fortitude	*159*
Questions and Answers about Fortitude	160
Justice	*164*
Questions and Answers about Justice	166
Temperance	*170*
Questions and Answers about Temperance	173
Faith	*185*
Questions and Answers about Faith	186
Hope	*195*
Questions and Answers about Hope	196
Love	*201*
Questions and Answers about Love	207
A Final Word	*212*

In these two volumes, I lay it all out for you: how your mind works, the seven sins that come from your mind and hold you back and the seven virtues in your soul that can be a source of joy and growth. Love is the greatest of the virtues because when you love, you accept everyone and everything around you. Love makes you stronger than you ever dreamed of. It makes you so strong that nothing can shake you. If that sounds like the life you want to live, then please join me.

Volume One: Sins

Introduction

Sins and virtues. They aren't words we use much anymore, and many people don't take them seriously. But as a matter of fact, ethics is more relevant today than ever. And when someone tells me that ethics aren't relevant to them because what they really need is to learn how to earn more money, I just shake my head.

In this book, I will show you how your success depends on your understanding of right and wrong. This is the information you need to prosper.

Don't believe me? Many people don't. At least, not at first. If I ran a poll on social media right now asking people what they need in order to attain prosperity, the answers would probably look something like this: you need to work harder, read the right books, network more, expand your horizons, improve your appearance, learn to persevere through challenges. The list goes on and on. We've all heard this advice before, and it's all true. To an extent.

But most of us—I'd say 99% of people—overlook the most important factors in becoming successful. One of them is something I've talked and written about before: your mood. Your mood is crucial in determining what happens to you. If you're in a bad mood, you won't get the results you want, no matter how hard you try. And yet people neglect to consider its impact. When you take care of your mood, the world around you and the people around you are happy.

Now, it's time to talk about a few more things that most people never think about: temptations, good intentions, and ethics. Those three things are literally the foundation of your life. They make you who you are inside. You can learn to say all the right words, and you can use my methods to build up a source of positivity inside yourself, and those things will help you attract people to whatever you want to accomplish. But if your values aren't where they need to be, they will act like a magnet and attract all the wrong people and wrong situations into your life. No matter how well you sell or how educated you are, you will never achieve the results you desire if your soul walks in darkness.

But people don't want to talk about this stuff. It's 'too deep.' Everyone wants to change their lives on the surface. I don't look at the surface. I always dig down to the root of the problem.

That's what this book is about.

Maybe philosophy was never your thing and you're wondering, "How is a book on ethics going to help me change my life?" You'll just have to believe me: this will help. It is the only thing that will.

I've spent many years writing books, giving consultations, and offering people life hacks and advice. I've watched people follow my advice and achieve what they wanted, and I've been proud of them. But I've also seen a lot of people follow my advice to the letter and not quite make it. So, I've watched them and thought about it and realised what's keeping them back: they're holding onto a negative quality like envy or resentment or even something as simple as laziness. Those qualities weigh a lot. They're heavy to carry around. And they create a mental block that prevents you from impacting the world the way you wanted.

So, this book is all about deep change.

Together, we'll look at the inner workings of the human soul. The dark side and the bright side. We'll figure out where our positive and negative impulses come from, and we'll make a list of everything we find. I don't have a list ready for you. We're going to make it together. I'll share with you the stories of people I've met, and we'll use those stories to discover exactly how the soul works and how to make it work better.

Did you know that I read people? In person or from a photograph—it doesn't matter. People used to bring me photographs and ask me, "Is this a good person? Can I trust this person?" And when I looked at the person's face, I could tell you everything about them. I could see their souls. If I saw these three particular negative qualities, then I knew what kind of life that person lived. And I knew what would happen to them if they didn't work on those negative qualities. If I saw positive qualities, I could tell what the person was capable of and how their life would turn out. Because under all the things we can control—how we dress, how we talk, how we behave—there is a matrix of positive and negative qualities that comes straight from the soul. And our job—if we want positive change in our lives—is to free ourselves from those negatives and develop our positives. That's the road to growth that I've never talked about before.

If you picked up this book and are prepared to trust me after reading this far, then thank you. You won't be disappointed with the results.

I listen to what nature tells me and to what I feel inside. That's just how I am. For this book, everything told me to start with the negatives. You may not enjoy it at first, but keep reading. These are the qualities you need to let go of. We will move on to the positive qualities after we drag out and examine the dark side of the soul, but in Part I we will focus on sins, fears, and other ugly traits. All the resentments, complexes, temptations, and vanity we pick up along the way and forget to put down. Just so you know, I never studied theology or psychology. But I see these qualities in people and think deeply about how their lives are affected. It's a deep subject. I'm going to work hard to make each quality comprehensible, and then I'll show you what it looks like in everyday life, how it can help you, how it can hurt you, and what to do if you need to get rid of it. Let's get started!

Pride

We could start anywhere, but I decided to keep it simple and start with the seven deadly sins. You've probably heard of the name, and you may even have seen the full list somewhere. Here it is, if you haven't seen it before: pride, envy, anger, lust, greed, despair, and gluttony. Even though most of us have heard of the concept of seven deadly sins, few people can list them all. We often use them in conversation without understanding what they mean and where they come from.

I strongly believe that if more people understood even just the definitions of those seven words, they would live happier lives and the world would be a better place. So, this is where we have to start.

First on the list is pride. For the purposes of this section, when I say 'pride,' I mean unhealthy pride, not the positive emotion that celebrates true accomplishment.

So, what is negative pride, anyway?

I don't want to just hand you a definition, and I don't want you looking it up online. Instead, I want you to close this book, grab a piece of paper and a pencil, and write down how you understand the word 'pride,' using your own words and without trying to impress anyone. Then come back here and we'll keep talking.

And please don't skip ahead. I want you to get the greatest possible benefit from this book, and that means setting it down right now and taking a moment to express your understanding of pride. Because if I give you my definition of the word before you think about it, you'll lose your own original vision of what pride means. Take a moment to think about it. Don't look for hints online. Write down what pride is and how you think it causes people to behave. Once you're done, you can keep reading.

(I'll be right here when you get back.)

Now that you're back, we can keep going.

If you look at the dictionary definition of pride, you'll see more than one explanation. Because there are two kinds of pride. There is unhealthy pride, which we will be focusing on because of all the ways it can hold you back and keep you from feeling unfulfilled, and there's healthy pride, which is fuelled by your joy in your own accomplishments and the accomplishments of the people around you. If I'm a martial arts trainer and my student wins a tough competition, what I'm feeling is healthy pride. It's a positive, warm feeling. Unhealthy pride doesn't come with that warmth and satisfaction. If I have unhealthy pride, I think that I'm smarter than all the people I work with. I don't believe in anything but myself. The Tibetans described it as having a corrupted mind, an unclean mind. Remember: when we talk about pride in this chapter, we're talking about negative, unhealthy pride.

The first thing, I want you to understand is that pride is more than outward behaviour. It's more than just talking about yourself and sharing your ideas. I've had readers send me messages complaining that I talk about myself too much in my books, and my standard response is: hey, my books are about me and the things I think about, so that's only natural. The unhealthy pride we're learning about right now, though, is something that sits inside a person and causes trouble. I can feel pride in a person's inner energy. People with unhealthy pride don't respect others. They don't believe in God. They think they are the centre of the universe and everyone else is crap. That's the energy I feel in people with a lot of unhealthy pride. Those are the ideas they have in their subconscious minds. People who are eaten up by pride don't believe in anything but their own minds. They think they're better and smarter than everyone else. They think they're in charge of everything. Imagine an atheist who believes that he has to fight everyone and shout everyone down or he won't get what he wants.

When people are eaten up by pride that way, they can't understand what it means to treat someone fairly or to act according to their conscience. They're like people without souls who run around wanting to succeed at everything and always be in the centre of attention. Even close family and friends are just tools for getting what they want from life. It's no surprise they try to make friends with important people so they can name-drop, not because they want a real relationship. You could call it being egotistical or conceited. There are a lot of words that describe this behaviour, so I'll give you several examples so you understand what I'm talking about.

Here's the first example: let's say I text a celebrity and ask if they want to go somewhere with me and hang out. A person who doesn't suffer from unhealthy pride will decide if they are interested in me and want to go, and if they have time to go, and let me know their situation. But a proud person is a superstar in their own mind, so they will reply in a way that shows me how important they are and how small I am. In between the lines, their meaning is: "Do you know who I am?" If a person acts like that all the time, that's unhealthy pride.

Don't get me wrong: sometimes even the best, kindest people have to set boundaries. If you're a hardworking professional with a high level of expertise and a colleague or client keeps questioning your judgment, you may have to say, "Look, please don't forget who you're talking to." But you aren't saying that out of pride. You just need the person to listen to you for their own good.

Talking about your achievements and your qualifications doesn't mean you have unhealthy pride. Because remember, pride is something inside you. You can talk about yourself all the time, as long as you understand there are forces greater than you in the universe, and as long as you let your conscience lead in your dealings with people. The difference is inside your heart.

You can't always rely on the words people use to figure out who in your life is acting from a place of unhealthy pride. If you just listen to their words, people can fool you. Clever people who are motivated by unhealthy pride will tell you they love you. Imagine that you're dating someone who lavishes you with attention and words of praise, but when they talk about the other people in their life, it's always the same story: your significant other is a saint who always gets treated badly by everyone around them. On the other hand, there are plenty of wise, generous people who will sometimes tell you things you don't want to hear or use language you don't like. One example would be a coach who pushes you to do your best but doesn't praise you all the time. Don't be fooled. Don't be attracted to a shiny exterior.

I'm giving you multiple examples to make sure you understand who you're dealing with when you encounter people suffering from unhealthy pride, so here's another example: imagine that the person suffering from pride is a journalist. He's popular, his work gets published everywhere, and he has a big presence on social media because he needs the audience. He makes his money by being out there and being available to people. He loves it when people interact with him in ways that are profitable to him, but he won't ever be your real friend. And if you see him at a live event and go up to shake hands and snap a selfie with him, afterwards he'll walk away and tell his friends of the moment what a piece of crap you are. That's how it works. You won't see him do it, but I see it and I know what it's all about. The journalist in my example has a bad case of unhealthy pride. He has no respect for his audience or for the other journalists who are his colleagues. The way he sees it, he's everything and they're nothing.

Unhealthy pride grows in people for a range of reasons. There are lots of seeds that cultivate it. Why do prideful people behave in negative ways? The primary reason is because they are insecure. Confident people don't expect everyone to bow down to them. They treat others like equals. So, the prideful person has insecurities. Now add in egotism, because people with unhealthy pride don't believe in God, and yet they want everything to be exactly how they think it ought to be. One of the first things they want is money. So, greed—the overwhelming desire for material goods—is part of the mix, too. And it's a vicious circle, because prideful people feel like they always have to prove how wonderful they are so they can get their hands on the money they can't live without. As a result, they are insecure about themselves, and they are always competing with you and everyone else in their lives. A prideful person is a person without faith. A person who keeps their eyes on this world.

I would go so far as to say that a prideful person is a victim of society. Why? Because I believe that if society didn't exist, then the prideful person would not be chasing after their desires constantly. They wouldn't be fuelled by pride because there would be no point. Pride only exists in a group, when the prideful person is surrounded by other people they can compare themselves to. When they see other people succeeding. When they feel like they have to compete. And that's where envy comes in. Envy is what you feel when you want something that other people have and you don't. So, envy is another component of unhealthy pride. That makes pride very interesting in the list of sins, doesn't it? It's the first one on our list, and seems to contain so many of the other negative traits.

Let's look at what we've arrived at so far: a prideful person is a person without faith, who lives by their own understanding, and who is corrupted by society. A person with an empty soul.

Now, let me give you an example of the opposite type of person. Imagine a young girl who knows nothing about what's going on in the world. When she goes outside to play, she is amazed by the sunrise or sunset. She loves looking at all the trees and how different they are. She watches people and enjoys the things that make them unique. And she just observes. If she goes into a store, she doesn't need to buy anything. She just enjoys seeing all the things on display. If she goes into an art gallery, she delights in the artists' paints and brushes. She has her own inner world, and it's a rich one.

When she comes home after school, she might take her camera outside and take pictures of people. She might sit down with a book. She might even write a book of her own. She could listen to music or play with a friend who has the same deep inner life. They're in a fairy tale together, and things just kind of magically happen. They aren't chasing after anything. Maybe someone at school notices their talent, and they get to go to Paris for a special event. And a few years later, the girl—now a young woman—meets a young man with a woodworking shop and they start making cool things together. Then the young man gets offered projects doing creative work for a company headquartered on a tropical island, so the girl goes with him and they end up living there.

All of that happened without the girl making any plans. She didn't care that the other girls at her school had more expensive clothes and backpacks. She didn't keep track of who was dating whom and what kind of cars the other girls' boyfriends drove. Maybe her boyfriend still doesn't have a car. She doesn't care, because she isn't prideful. She isn't corrupted by the world around her. She chooses the things in her life based on her own judgment. She's the artist behind her own life. She's pure. That's an example of a person with faith.

People without faith are left to live by their pride. A prideful woman worries about all the things her friends' husbands have that her husband doesn't have. Do you see how it works? Pride is a knotted collection of negative characteristics and temptations.

We all are born with positive and negative characteristics, but how we turn out depends on how we choose to live. Some people are able to look within and turn things around, and other people end up with a laundry list of negative personality traits by the time they are in high school or college. You've probably experienced or heard of children getting bullied for being poor or being of a different race. Kids can be cruel. A lot of the insecurities that people live with have their roots in schoolyard trauma, and those feelings of insecurity and psychological distress can give rise to prideful behaviour. A person feels like crap for not carrying the right backpack or living in the right neighbourhood. Later on, they have those negative feelings because they don't have the right car or vacation in the best places. It just goes on and on.

Social media—especially Instagram—is the devil's temptation. People with pure hearts can use the internet and social media for good, but for young people who are still finding themselves, social media can keep them from knowing their own soul and finding their foundation in life. Instead, they lose their spark and fall prey to mental illness. I'm sure you're familiar with examples. You've seen these people. Maybe you've felt some of these things, yourself.

Later on in this book, we will look at some ways to overcome unhealthy pride. But I'll give you the short answer here: you have to turn off your mind. All the negative ingredients that go into pride come from the mind. So, if we turn off the mind, we stop feeding the pride. I've talked about other ways to deal with negative traits in my books and videos, and I'll go into that here, too, but first I want to answer some of the questions that people are always asking me. My answers to these questions are all based on examples from real life, because once you see how pride works in the people around you, your own pride and your own mind will lose some of their hold on you. Each example I'm about to give you will help you understand unhealthy pride even deeper. I'm spending a lot of time on this because I don't want you to be confused about which actions are wrong and sinful and which aren't.

Question and Answers about Pride

Question: Alex, you say that prideful people don't believe in God. Does that mean that it's a sin to be an atheist?

That's exactly what I'm saying. Being prideful means relying only on your own mind. A prideful person doesn't believe in God or any type of higher power. Instead, they only believe in their own strength and their own mind. That's a bad thing, naturally. What's funny is that I hear lots of public figures, journalists, bloggers, and the like talk about being atheists as if that was something to be proud of. There's nothing wonderful about it. I'd say it's a terrifying place to be.

Question: Are there different levels of pride?

Of course. Some people are more prideful than others. I can't give you precise numbers, but there's definitely a spectrum. Almost everyone has a little bit of it, but some people try to keep it in check while others don't care. They just walk all over the people around them. That's the only difference.

Question: What should a person do if they are surrounded by prideful people at home and at work?

If you're at work, then you just have to deal with it. You have to learn to have a strong spirit. Although let me qualify that. If I saw that my friend was affected by prideful people at work, then I would advise him to quit and find another job. But if I saw that same friend surrounded by prideful people at work and keeping his head on his shoulders, not letting himself be influenced, knowing his worth, and knowing his place, then I wouldn't worry about him. He isn't going to be tempted. He has a strong spirit. I've never been affected by people who have negative traits like unhealthy pride. It just doesn't touch me. If I was weaker, I would become like them. But I have the opposite problem because I'm hypersensitive. I feel all the negative energy of their pride, all of the dirt and grime, even if it doesn't change how I behave. I hate feeling that way, so I do my best to stay away from those people. So, my answer about dealing with negative people at work is this: remember that prideful people are everywhere. It isn't worth quitting your job.

If the prideful people around you are your relatives, then it's important to see the value in that relationship. Our relatives are given to us so we can compare ourselves to them and learn from them within a relationship. When we learn from the strengths and weaknesses we see in our families, we can better understand the other people we meet in the world. So, don't turn away from your relatives just because they are prideful.

Question: Alex, what about my preacher at church? Could he be suffering from unhealthy pride?

Of course, he could. Preachers are humans. Just like doctors and politicians and teachers and everyone else. That's why they say that humans are sinful. If you want a per cent, then 99.9% of all humans are suffering from pride. The handful of people who are pure might as well be aliens from another planet.

Question: Prideful people are just ashamed to ask for help, aren't they?

I disagree with that. A prideful person doesn't just feel uncomfortable admitting that they need help. Negative, harmful pride makes you an egotist. It cuts you off from belief in anything but the power of your own mind. Prideful people aren't just hard workers who feel bad if someone tries to give them a hand; they actually want to bend others to their will. Being too proud to accept help is an entirely different issue. People with unhealthy pride will not be ashamed to use and exploit the people around them.

Question: What are the negative consequences of being prideful? Is pride punished in this life?

As I've already explained, if you have unhealthy pride, you only believe in your own mind. You don't believe in God, and you are cut off from your own life. You don't have a guardian angel. You don't have a source of energy. You aren't connected to nature. Nothing controls you. If I'm driving a remote-control car, I steer it around all the obstacles and puddles in its path. The car is safe and dry. I'm like God for that car. We all are like little cars that don't want to allow God to direct us. Instead, we run around wherever we want. When a car doesn't have a driver, it becomes responsible for its own life. And a person running their own life will drown if they don't navigate safely. When you allow God to direct you and trust him, then you can be at peace. You know that your car will safely drive around the puddles. You aren't in charge. You are being controlled from above. Those are two very different ways to live.

You asked if pride is punished. Prideful people are constantly tested, and their lives are plagued by difficulties and obstacles that attempt to beat that pride out of them. This isn't punishment. It's just nature's way of trying to beat that pride out of you. So, that's one negative consequence of living with unhealthy pride in your heart.

Another consequence is that other prideful people will be attracted to you. Like attracts like. There are exceptions, of course, but generally people end up surrounded by others who are like them. When I've helped people clean up their hearts and turn their lives around, I always tell them not to be in a hurry to get into a serious romantic relationship. I tell them to get themselves clean first. Here's how I explain it: if you're 20% dirty inside, then any person you become involved with will be at that same level. But if you wait and continue to cleanse your heart and get to where you're only 10% dirty inside, then the person you meet will be cleaner, too. That's an important thing to consider.

Another consequence of being prideful is that you're always bored and dissatisfied. Nothing astonishing or wonderful can happen to you because you maintain tight control. You always have to be in charge. And you don't notice the amazing opportunities that come your way, maybe in your personal life or in your career, because you don't keep your eyes and your heart open. You already think you're smarter than everyone else. So, you lose out on all that potential. People complain that they don't get the right opportunities in life, but the truth is that the opportunities were always there. You just turned away from them.

Question: Should I not talk to people about my achievements? Will that keep me from becoming proud?

Not at all. I've been getting harassed online for years by people who tell me I shouldn't talk about my success. But that's a mistaken understanding of pride. Talking about your actual achievements doesn't make you a bad person. It doesn't make you prideful. Say you're a star athlete, say in football, tennis, or hockey, or you built a new satellite, or you published an important book, or you painted a whole bunch of paintings that are now in museums around the world. You have every right to point to that achievement and say, "Look at what I did! I'm proud of myself!" If I'm an artist and my paintings are selling for millions of dollars and there are articles about me in all the magazines, then I can say that with an absolutely pure heart. That's not boasting. What matters is the intent.

The motivation. That's why it can be hard for many people to distinguish between someone who is boasting and someone who is legitimately proud of their accomplishments. The words may sound the same. If you've achieved something, don't worry—go right ahead and tell people about it. As long as your goal isn't to make others feel bad. If it's sincere and pure, then there's nothing wrong with speaking out about who you are and what you've done. There's nothing wrong with healthy pride.

If I meet a new person tomorrow and they ask me what I do, I can tell them that I've written multiple books, that I do consulting, that I'm working on a bunch of projects, that I own land and real estate, that I have a certain number of people working for me, that I have millions of dollars in the bank. And if that person gets offended because they think I'm bragging, who is the problem? They are, not me. But only because I am speaking sincerely like a child who didn't know that people can find your success upsetting. If I was exaggerating or trying to attract attention, that would make me prideful. But if I'm just calmly telling someone the truth about my life, there's absolutely nothing wrong with that. It's not my fault if that person feels insecure or envious about my success.

The opposite can also be true. If you see someone selling themselves on social media and talking about how much money they have and how important they are, then that's pride. That person is tempting others, trying to attract their attention to material things. They're boasting. And they're going to pay for it. Maybe they'll get cancer or some other disease. You can almost predict the timing. Less than five years later, you'll see the news. And it's all because their intentions are not pure. But if you have child-like sincerity, your intentions are pure, and you're just explaining who you are and what you can do, then there's nothing wrong with that. That's not a sin.

I know it's hard for many people to tell the difference when they listen to someone talking about themselves. Are they boasting or not? I can usually feel the difference. When someone talks about their achievements, I can feel if they are calm inside or if they are just churning with a need to be seen. When people are boasting, their souls are agitated. That's pride working. When they're just explaining themselves, their souls are at peace. You have to learn to spot the difference.

Question: What is the difference between wanting to be better than everyone around you and simply wanting to live a better life? Where is the boundary between prideful behaviour and bettering yourself?

This is an excellent question because you already see that the difference is all about intent. If you suffer from harmful pride, you want to have an expensive car because it will make you feel better about your insecurities and your envy. You want to find a spouse who is good-looking and wealthy to make you look better in other people's eyes. You want a house on the beach so everyone can see how successful you are. Harmful pride makes you feel all hollow inside when you see that someone else has something you don't have. You feel like crap. That's harmful pride. That's insecurity. At least 50% of people are infected by it.

If you don't have a problem with harmful pride, you want a better car so you and whoever rides with you will be safer and more comfortable, or maybe so you'll have room for all your kids. You want to live in a better neighbourhood so your kids can go to better schools and be around people who work hard and do their best. You want a house with a view of the mountains or the ocean or the big city because you enjoy looking at it. Do you see the difference? That's an entirely different set of intentions. You have a sincere desire and you've considered it calmly. You don't get a churning feeling in the pit of your stomach when you think about the thing you want. You simply want a better life. There is nothing sinful about that.

Even relatively small material things can reveal your values. For a lot of young people, high school and college is a time of temptation. They see people who have more money than they do or simply spend their money in different ways. Even something as simple as a new bag can feel like a huge decision. Do you buy an affordable bag that's big enough to fit your laptop? Or do you buy the expensive designer bag that people will notice? The one that will look good in the photos you post to social media? So, you see, temptation can be present even in the small things. Every time you make a choice, you risk falling into the void. I know this will be controversial, but I believe women fall prey to their pride more often than men. We will talk about the origins of that in the Bible later. For now, I just want you to remember that temptation is built into society. It's everywhere. Maybe you bought your house not because it was in a good location for your family, but because it was in a prestigious location. Or you pick a car that doesn't do everything you need, but it screams "I have money!" when you drive it down the street. If I make ten choices this week, those are ten opportunities to let my pride turn me away from my soul. But if I make the right choices, those become ten opportunities to strengthen my soul and take power away from my pride. That's exactly how it works. Temptation is always waiting for you. Every time you choose how to spend your money or your time. Do I hang out with those friends, or with these other friends? Do I buy a new shirt, or do I save the money for something important?

Question: Can what you call harmful pride ever play a positive role in my life?

That's an interesting question, and that's really what this whole book is about. Once you understand the answer to that question, you'll understand how everything works. Pride, negative personality traits, everything. And once you understand those things, you'll already be free of at least half of the crap holding you back. At the very least, you'll be regaining control of your life.

Can harmful pride play a positive role in your life? It can. I take this topic seriously because of something that happened to me that still gives me goosebumps. It was early 2010, so I hadn't met any of the messengers yet or the man who would become my mentor. Every kid is supposed to be pretty much like every other kid, but I suddenly realised I was a super genius. I know how that sounds, but it's true. I realised that I was a super genius. That I could see right through people. I was just 19 years old, but I realised I could start any business or get any job I wanted. I could be anyone's best friend. That's how calm and confident I was. But here's the thing: I didn't want to. I couldn't see why I should bother. I didn't feel the need to buy a car, for example. I didn't need money because there wasn't anything I wanted to spend it on. People kept telling me I should work hard and make more money. But why bother? I didn't want to buy a place to live if I could cover my rent by photographing people. Or I could play some poker and make rent that way. I felt like if I needed to raise a certain amount of cash, say $2,000, I could just sit down and come up with 100 ways to get the money in under a week. If I needed $20,000, then that was just a different number. I could still raise the money in a week, I'd just have to do slightly different things to get it. I showed my friends how it worked so many times, but they never understood. They thought that if I could make money that easily I should keep on doing it all the time. But I didn't want to bother if I had no needs at the moment. That right there—not needing anything—was hard for people to get their heads around. I started meeting people who were making serious money, and I just couldn't understand their motivation. Their obsession with money didn't make sense to me. Now, I understand: they were letting their insecurities control them and dictate their values. Their negative traits were in charge. They were tempted by greed. And people like that do well materially and socially. I didn't have those qualities, and there was nothing I could do about it. I could do the same thing if I wanted to: I could turn off my feelings and just put my head down and work. But they do it without realising what they're doing because they're blinded by all those negative traits. Their negative characteristics force them in a certain direction and force them to succeed. If you took away their pride and their other problems, they wouldn't be able to make themselves do anything. They would just freeze.

When a person is not mindful, they end up being driven by their negative traits. Temptations keep them moving and striving. Temptations make them angry at others.

I didn't have any of those characteristics. I was standing outside in the hall, so to speak. So, I just kept writing my books. But slowly, I began to realise that I had it all backward. Those other people weren't doing better than me. I could see that they had a lot of negative characteristics, but I couldn't understand why I was born without any of those traits, like a big zero. They might be cheating each other and competing against each other, but at least they were similar in a lot of ways. It felt like the world belonged to them, not to me. I was strange. The odd one out. But then I realised that that's the first level of awareness. The first level of awareness is where you let go of all those character flaws. You're as pure as a big zero, but you still don't have the instructions you need for living as a zero. Over time, you understand that you won't work if you don't make yourself work. You won't go out and meet people if you don't force yourself to do it.

Life is different for people who are controlled by their character flaws. They experience everything as emotion. When they see a successful person, they have a burning desire to go up and introduce themselves. If they buy expensive things, they feel driven to go where they can show those things off. They post photos for likes and comments. They need attention. But since I was a zero, I didn't care about any of that. So, why do I post photos? Just because. Other people act based on impulses from their negative traits, but I don't have those impulses. And since I'm mindful, I do what I need to do without any emotion. Now, for the most interesting part. This is addressed to my long-time readers, the people who have read my books and participated in my discussion groups where I explained that you have to turn off your mind and turn on your inner self and become mindful. And you loved it. You told me you wanted personal growth. You told me you'd spent your whole lives looking for meaning, visiting the Hari Krishnas and the special places of strength, all the highest mountains, and you told me that I gave you what you'd been seeking so many years. Awareness. And I gave it to you. But you didn't know what you were asking for! You wanted awareness, but did you know what the consequences would be? Did you understand what life would be like when nothing tempts you and you just sit around at home? Are you surprised at how bored you feel sometimes? Let me explain: it's because you freed yourself from all of society's crap, all the things that society uses to get you out of your house. Now you have to come up with your own reasons to leave the house. That's the cool thing. That's awareness.

Let me take a different tack for a minute. Someone recently asked me how I would feel if one of my employees decided to go out on their own and start their own business after I've invested in them, introduced them to people, taught them, given them gifts even. And I said, "I'd be fine with that. I'm not going to try to hold someone back if they've grown beyond what they do for me." But then they asked me, "What if you just recently hired them or just promoted them? How would you feel then?" And my response was, "That's a totally different story. In that case, they'd be in the wrong." The way I see it, a mindful person is going to want to repay my investment in them before they move on to something else. But I thought it was an interesting question, so I want to go into it in more detail.

I see many people who are bothered by working for someone else. It gets to them that someone else is the boss, because they want to be in charge. I started to think about why that is. Let's say, I work for a company that builds boats. My boss is the one who opened the company, and I work for him. He taught me everything I know, and I'm glad to have the job. If I have no insecurities or egoism, then it doesn't bother me when magazines do features about my boss. It doesn't bother me that he has a lot of money. Because I know my place and I respect my employer. But many people don't feel that way about their jobs. Instead, they think, "There's nothing special about him. I'm the one actually making the boats. I want to be in charge, too." That's just one example of a serious sin.

Here's another example from my real life. I met a young guy who was working as a graphic designer and earning almost nothing. So, I introduced him to a friend of mine, and that friend gave him a job. Suddenly, this small-town kid was making three times more money and doing projects for big name clients he never could have gotten before. But what happened next? His egoism and his pride got to him. He started to resent the man that hired him for two reasons: because he was the face of the company and got all the attention, and because he kept a percentage of the fees for all the jobs this kid was doing. So, the kid decided to be his own boss, and he took the portfolio of work he had been doing for his employer and started showing it to people like it was all his own work. As if he had gone out and found all those clients on his own. Just imagine how foolish he looked. That kind of pride makes you stupid. Someone was giving that kid work and paying him three times more for it than he'd ever made before, and all he could think was, "Why am I not the boss?"

Some people are even willing to make less money if they can boast about being in charge. They want to have a business card with the big title and the big company on it. You could offer a person like that a six-figure salary to do a less prestigious job, and they will choose the prestige every time. They would rather be a cog in a huge corporation than open their own business, even if it means making less money. For some people, the draw is political power. They'll work as a legislative assistant for next to nothing just to say they're in the legislature.

A lot of my readers are turned off when I explain how this works. They don't want to hear about temptations and sin. If I announced that I'd be teaching people how to fly, they'd get in line to sign up. They want to hear about harnessing the energy of the sun. Or making money. Or working miracles. They don't want to know about their own character flaws.

When you're shocked to realise that you're with the wrong person, or when you're shocked that something you bought isn't what you thought it would be, know that your pride blinded you. You chose the wrong romantic partner because of pride. Being prideful changes your values. You see things differently. And you start to make mistakes. Conclusion: if you want to be confident about the choices you make in life, first you need to cleanse yourself of your pride. Then you'll be drawn to the truth. As long as you're controlled by pride, you'll keep making the wrong choices. Prideful people are infuriated by my social media presence. They're infuriated by my name: The King. They're angry because the grime in their souls makes them angry. Because they want to be important, too. And they get even angrier when they read all the comments on my posts where people share how much they love my message. Some feel like they just have to write me and say something nasty. Do you know how funny that is?

I want to repeat myself a little bit here to make sure you understand. Many of the character flaws we've talked about are the very things that keep people moving. That's how society is set up. If you're insecure, you work on your appearance. If you're confident, you don't care how you look. Greed makes a person competitive instead of lazy. He literally can't sit still because of his greed and envy. Sometimes, you have to be mature enough to understand this.

You probably have a lot of questions at this point. Are you thinking, "But don't positive character traits motivate people, too?" or "What if a person doesn't have any character flaws? What motivates them?" We will get to that in a little bit. Pride is the first sin we looked at closely. I hope you understand that unhealthy pride is made up of a variety of negative traits that feed pride and build it up. We will look at each trait individually, too, at a later point in the book. First, I want to explain each of the six other sins and give you examples to think about.

Your mind is growing and becoming more flexible, and I hope that gives you a sense of enlightenment about how the world works. Now that you understand, you'll have better insight into your children's behaviour, your own reactions to situations, and why the people around you behave the way they do. You'll understand the true cause and effect of each action.

When I look at a person, my reaction is usually just one word, and that one word sums up what I see in them. If you show me a photo of someone, I can tell you if they are a leader or a coward, a thief or a liar. I can see their character flaws, the things that motivate them. And once I've found that character flaw, I can describe exactly how that person is successful and what trouble they run into. I can tell them about all the problems they're going to have in the near future. People are usually in shock. "How do you know so much about me?" It's all science. It's all math. There are no miracles. People just can't see it. Even the Bible—the most popular book—explains the algorithm that controls the world and human life. If people weren't so superficial, if they took the time to read every word in the Bible the way I'm explaining it to you, they would achieve success and be happy.

Envy

We made it to the next sin on the list: envy. Sounds obvious, doesn't it? We usually think of envy as wanting something that someone else has. But sit down and think about your own personal definition of envy, because the act of considering that question is important for your mental growth. My goal here is to help you clean out your mind so it becomes more flexible and stops getting in your way. So, take a moment and write down who you feel envious of and why. Think of it as an exercise like writing in a diary. Don't be afraid to admit that you experience envy: the sooner you recognise your negative traits, the sooner you can free yourself from them. If you try to hide those parts of yourself, if you don't accept yourself the way you are, then you can actually start moving backward.

While you're writing, consider exactly how you feel when you experience envy. I know that when I'm around someone who is envious, I can smell it on them. It's an unpleasant odour. Think about all the bloggers who post content that tempts you to envy. I don't want to offend anyone, so I won't name any names. You know the content I mean: they show you their cars and their money, or their beautiful homes and well-dressed kids, or their travels to exotic places, and they talk about how amazing their lives are. Pay attention to how you feel when you look at that content. You probably aren't angry at the person in the video for having those things. You probably don't want to take those things away from them. It's more like you start to hate yourself for not having the same things. You feel like a loser. That's envy, too. Envy comes in different forms. Sometimes, you hate yourself for not having certain things. Or you might want to take away something that someone else has. Or you wish you could copy the success that someone else has. So, think about all those different types of envy and write down your thoughts and experiences. Once you're done, you'll be ready to hear and understand what I'm going to tell you about envy.

Questions and Answers about Envy

Question: Is there such a thing as 'good envy?'

Envy is always a bad thing, but not every comparison you make is envy. You might see someone and say, "I'm glad that she has that object or achieved that success. Someday I'll have that object or achieve that success for myself." There's nothing wrong with feeling that way. That isn't envy. Envy is about what you feel inside, so when your emotions are positive, you aren't experiencing envy. The negative traits we look at in this book are based on feelings, not on words. If someone wins first prize, or achieves something, or has a strong family, and you look at that and are happy for them, then you aren't envious. Envy is like an instinct—like a feeling you can't control.

Question: What causes envy?

The roots of envy are in your mind. If you were confident and enjoying your life, would you envy others? No. If you were fulfilled, would you be envious? Of course not. Envy is what people feel when they don't love and accept themselves. The material conditions of your life don't matter. A person can be satisfied with very little as long as their heart is pure. He accepts his family the way it is and doesn't judge his relatives. She accepts herself the way she is and does the things she enjoys doing. If she likes playing sports, she plays sports. If she wants to read, she reads. If he needs to earn money, he goes to work and earns it.

People like that are not tempted by society. They don't care how other people live. Society has this frequency where it vibrates and radiates temptations, and the people who avoid that frequency don't suffer from envy. Pure people stick to their own spiritual frequency, so they are simply incapable of feeling envy. Here's an important point: envy doesn't happen to poor people. There are plenty of people out there who have less than most of my readers, and they don't go around feeling envious. Envy has nothing to do with your finances, your personal belongings, or your career, and it has everything to do with how you tend your soul.

People who are sincere with themselves and others, who live according to their true hearts, have no envy. Envious people are the ones that have lost their souls or sold them. They're the people who have turned away from their own hearts. And the more they give in to temptation, the stronger their envy becomes. How does a person first get infected with envy? Well, they might fall in with the wrong group of friends. People who encourage them to be dishonest and cheat others. Or to be disrespectful of those around them. Or to betray a friend to get something they want. People who push you to do those kinds of things are like demons. They are tempting you. And the more you go along with it, the more negative character traits you end up with, including envy. If you stay away from social and material temptations, however, you will not fall prey to envy.

It is not easy to ignore those social and material temptations. If I took you to lunch with a group of highly successful business people who live according to society's rules, you would feel them sizing you up, figuring out who you are and what you're worth. It's a really unpleasant sensation. They won't say anything bad about you. They'll pretend to be glad to meet you. But in reality, they write you off because they think you're less important than they are.

If, on the other hand, I took you to lunch with a group of people with pure hearts, they would accept you for who you are. Maybe you blush when you talk to strangers. Or your ears stick out. Or you say dumb things when you get nervous. It wouldn't matter: they would still accept you because they are pure inside, without all the crap that comes from temptation. Greed, insecurity, envy. So again, all those negative traits are interconnected.

Looking back on what we've uncovered here, can you see what feeds envy? One word: judgement. When you judge people, that gives rise to all the other negative characteristics. Even being judgemental toward yourself—looking outside at the world instead of inside to your heart—gives rise to envy. This is another area where social media can make it hard to focus on yourself. You see your friend taking an awesome vacation, or an influencer buying a fancy new car, or a minor celebrity having a party with her family, or someone showing off their material wealth and offering to teach others how to attain that same level of prosperity, and you feel envious. Even if you don't feel envious at first, the seeds of envy have been planted. All because you're more focused on other people's lives than on your own. Conversely, if you stop fixating on other people's lives and stop judging and comparing everyone, including yourself, your envy will lose power.

Resentment is another root cause of envy. Some people are just full of resentment. You have to understand that 100% of the time when you feel resentment toward someone—because they offended you somehow—the problem is inside of you. This is important, so I want you to remember it. If you accept yourself and accept the world the way it actually is, then you won't feel resentment. Instead, you'll be practicing tolerance. That's a positive quality we will talk about in the second half of the book. For right now, I want you to think of it in the context of resentment. If you practice tolerance, then you won't feel resentment, no matter what happens to you. Maybe the people around you are behaving badly, but you can stay above that if you're pure inside. If you clear out the crap in your heart, you won't go around feeling offended. Ninety-nine per cent of people who get offended bring it on themselves. They're so full of resentment that they're literally waiting for someone to hurt their feelings. No matter what the context, your resentment is your own problem. You bring it on yourself. Often people say that their resentment comes from all the bad things people have done to them. Here's what I say: if you didn't cultivate relationships with people who want to hurt you, then none of those bad things would happen.

Besides being a root cause of envy, resentment is a dangerous emotion in its own right. I often hear from readers who complain about someone in their life who hurt them or who offended them. I tell them that's an opportunity for growth. It frightens me when people say they have deep resentment against their mother or father. How can you be so filthy inside and so full of resentment that you can't forgive your own family for something? Instead, you let it rot inside you for decades. At least half of the people I work with as a coach have a story like that. It's unbelievable. You're wearing the devil's own glasses when you look at your relatives that way. Your parents belong to you and you to them—that's nature. Maybe you're a type of plant that blooms and smells good, and your parent is more like a prickly cactus. Accept that you were born into a cactus family. If you resent the cactus, that's your problem. You'll never change your relatives through resentment, and you'll never make life be fair. All you're doing is slowly killing yourself.

Like I explained before, these negative traits are interconnected, and one thing that envy feeds into is a lack of confidence. When you are envious, you feel like crap and your inner core is weakened. There are different kinds of envy, of course. Sometimes, envy can have the opposite effect, pushing you to achieve a goal to satisfy your greed or your need to show others that you're better than they are. Other people react to envious feelings by giving up and admitting defeat. So, all of these negative characteristics are linked.

Every person has a negative trait that is strongly expressed in their personality, and that single trait brings a host of other problems along with it. So, if you want to work on a negative trait, first you have to find the underlying cause and fix it. When you do that, you are essentially getting rid of two negative traits at the same time. And that can be the start of a virtuous cycle by which you remove even more problematic aspects of your personality.

That's how the human mind works. If you're starting to notice how many of these negative traits affect you, don't feel bad: everyone else has shortcomings they need to work on. They're just expressed differently in different people because the root cause is always specific to each individual. And don't forget that you and the rest of us have good qualities, as well. If you're committed to personal growth, you'll do your best to weed out your negative traits. The first step to growth is figuring out what underlying cause feeds your own negative traits and rooting it out so those traits die back. Then you can identify your positive characteristics and feed and encourage them. And because growth is a virtuous cycle, feeding your positive traits will cause even more positive traits to wake up and become active.

In this respect, your actions reflect your choices. When you choose growth, you behave in positive ways. When you choose weakness, your actions reinforce the very negative traits you want to get rid of and weaken your positive traits.

If you've spent time studying my theory of frequencies, you might spend a whole month experiencing only good, kind intentions. No lust, temptation, greed, resentment, or envy. Only love and faith. You feel pure and kind and wonderful. Heck, you don't just *feel* kind. You *are* kind. Maybe even for a whole year. And then something happens and—click—you're the same person, but you're suddenly full of negative traits clamouring for attention. You feel envious, you give in to temptation, and you tempt others to join you.

Do you see how that works? You can spend time on the bright side of life and time on the dark side. Being on the dark side doesn't mean that you're doomed. Just as being on the bright side right now is no guarantee. If you fall under the influence of the wrong person or the wrong group, you can behave in negative ways and become a demon. I have seen plenty of examples of that change. So, pay close attention to yourself and your friends. Maybe you had a friend who was a good, solid person, but when you run into them years later, they've changed. They're tearing people down on social media and promoting themselves everywhere to get attention. But you knew their good side. What happened? They fell under the influence of someone negative. It's much easier to be influenced by the negative traits of the people around you than by their positive traits. Being a good person is hard work. Letting yourself become an asshole is easy by comparison. So, people give in. Your friend probably tried for a while, they remembered how they were raised and tried to honour that, but in the end the bad influences in their life broke them down. That's how people describe it: being broken down by life. They surrender and become like the assholes they surrounded themselves with. They hung out with people who mistreated them, and then they reacted to that mistreatment by exacting revenge. And remember, revenge is a sin. A person who commits an act of revenge has turned away from their own soul. The fire in them is gone. All their good intentions and positive qualities are choked out and replaced by negative traits. That's how it works.

Question: Is jealousy a type of envy?

Yes, but there's more to it than that. You'll be amazed at how simple it all is. We've been talking about envy, and now there's this other negative trait that's come up—jealousy. Like resentment, jealousy is a negative trait that reveals a person's level of personal growth. Or lack thereof. A jealous person might be good and decent inside, but they have this weakness they haven't dealt with. When you start measuring who has the biggest dick, you're showing your weakness.

What is jealousy? It's an extension of your lack of confidence in yourself. If you felt like a fantastic person with a fantastic life, what cause would you have for jealousy? Jealous people are unaware; they live in a fog. Their relationships are not based on sincerity and trust. They don't truly understand the people around them. And so, they feel jealous. Just like envy, jealousy comes from a lack of confidence, from low self-esteem. Interestingly, a lack of confidence is behind many of the negative traits that cause us to suffer.

At its foundation, lack of confidence is lack of faith. The unconfident person has no faith in God and no faith in their own abilities. They don't believe in their own inner world, so they are always looking around to see how other people are living. And because they keep their eyes focused on others, they don't listen to their own soul. Instead, they judge themselves and the people around them. All of these negative traits—resentment, envy, jealousy—come from a basic lack of confidence. Jealous people live according to others' advice and others' gossip. They copy what others do.

Just recently, I received messages from three different musicians. Kind of a coincidence. And all three admitted to being envious of more successful musicians. That's no surprise. If I started looking around at other writers, paying attention to how many books they're selling, and comparing those numbers to my own, then I would start to feel like crap, too.

But I don't look to others to define my success. Great artists—musicians, directors, writers—never look to others. They live by the designs of their own hearts. A talented director doesn't look at how other directors make movies so they can do the same thing but better. A talented director makes their own movie. They show us their soul through a movie that is theirs alone. People may or may not agree with the director, but the director doesn't care.

How many people in today's world are strong enough to live by their own hearts? Not many. Most people are wrapped up in copying what others are doing, so naturally they feel envious. When you imitate others, you compare yourself to them. You see that they're doing great and you aren't, so you feel like crap. But try looking at it this way: if you're a musician, is your ultimate goal to beat all the other musicians? Of course not! Your goal is to make your own music. There's no point in following what other musicians are doing. Think about this long and hard. Don't be surprised when you look around at people and feel envious or unsure of yourself, but remember that you're the one creating those feelings.

If you want to be truly creative, stop watching other people. Don't look to society for inspiration. You have to live in your own world. You have to create that world and protect it. When you walk down the street, you aren't looking at what other people are doing so you can measure yourself against them. You just pick up on all the sights and sounds that inspire you. You check out all the musical instruments to see what they can do. That's a truly creative approach. That's what a creative person does. When you sit on a bench in the park, you aren't worrying about whether you live in a cool enough neighbourhood. You just write the music that comes from your heart. If your heart wants to go whale-watching, you go whale-watching. If your heart wants to climb mountains, you climb mountains. And the more you serve your heart and soul, the stronger they grow. But if you act like a fool and value everything you see other people doing, you lose that creativity. Most of the so-called creative content you see on social media is made to feed the algorithm, not your soul. You can either be a creative person or you can follow the algorithm; it's your choice.

Question: If someone in your life envies you, should you avoid that person?

It depends. If you can tell that a random person who isn't particularly close to you envies you, then ignore it. Let them envy you. That's none of your business. But be careful if it's someone closer to you. And here's another thing: it doesn't matter whether they envy you or someone else, just being around envious people can affect you. You start to vibrate on their frequency. So, be careful. It's like a virus. If I surround myself with people who want money and attention more than anything in the world, who don't respect their elders, who dream of sportscars, who envy everyone who has more money than they do, then I will eventually become like them. All the willpower in the world won't help me. Sooner or later, I'll soak up that envy and start to feel it. So, we have to avoid those people.

I've found myself in friend groups with envious people, especially when I was younger and didn't understand how it all works. I ended up leaving university to get away from materialism and envy. University is supposed to be a time of learning. You open your mind and grow as a person. But the students around me were more interested in talking about cars and money and sex that in learning anything. I saw young men treating young women as objects, and young women treating other young women as competitors for male attention. It isn't healthy to socialise with people like that, so I made the decision to leave.

So, you see, I had a choice. On the one hand, I was supposed to get my degree, but on the other hand, I didn't want to be around people who behaved like animals. So, I left. You will face choices, too, and sometimes you have to make the hard decision to leave a situation that isn't conducive to growth. I always avoid materialists because I don't want to risk becoming one of them.

Some people say that truly good people are few and far between. I disagree. They're out there, and the cleaner and more sincere you become, the more you'll attract other good people. And the negative people will avoid you. I'm serious. If I turned my feed into a source of temptation, with photos of me eating oysters with beautiful women then I'd gain a bunch of new followers from that world. But none of them would be interested in doing a retreat with me in Karelia. The people who are attracted by that kind of content don't want to sit quietly among the trees and think. They want to travel to places like London and Monaco where it's noisy and there are lots of distractions. When you're in Karelia, you sit on the bank of a river and fish. You go hiking with other people who love the woods. See how it works? When you do the things that matter to you, then slowly you grow a community of people who share those interests.

Here's another interesting question to think about: are you necessarily envious when you criticise someone? If you point out their faults, is it because you're envious? I say it depends on the feeling behind the words. If I mention that I don't like a particular singer, then I have a right to that opinion. But if I'm upset inside when I say it, then envy might be one of the reasons behind my criticism. We criticise the people we envy almost as a defensive mechanism, and it's usually obvious to those around us.

Again, that kind of envy is caused by a lack of confidence. You're angry because people are praising someone else instead of you. So, you tell yourself that the other person doesn't deserve that praise. Your pride wakes up because you think you're better than the other person, and your criticism is the outward symptom of what's going on in your mind. It's almost a mix of pride and envy, because you don't exactly want what that person has—you just don't want to hear other people praise them in front of you.

Question: Can envy be a motivator for personal growth?

I doubt it. Sure, I've seen plenty of cases where envy drove a person to exercise self-control and work hard. But they were stealing others' ideas and copying others. When you're fuelled by envy, everything you try to do is going to be affected by that. Even when you try to do the right thing. You can't achieve personal growth and positive change in your life when you're motivated by a force like envy, because envy causes you to measure your life by other people's definition of success. So, I would never call envy a good quality or a motivating factor.

I would go so far as to say that the kind of envy that makes you want to give up is preferable to the kind of envy that motivates you to compete with everyone. When you compare yourself to the people around you and feel defeated, that sense of failure gives you an opportunity to listen to your own heart. You have a chance to realize that you're being controlled by envy. But when envy energises you and motivates you to outdo everyone, you don't see that envy as a negative trait. There's nothing to stop you from falling deeper and deeper into temptation.

It's harder to reach the people who are motivated by envy. People whose envy makes them feel sad and depressed are easier to get through to. They can still hear their own inner voice. It's an interesting paradox.

Question: Do people join religious communities because they want to save their souls from temptation?

That's an interesting question, and it's worth diving deep into the answer. The theme of trying to save your own soul or your child's soul from temptation always gets distorted in the media and in movies. If you believe the media, the families that try to protect their children from society's values are all small-minded extremists who think that if a girl wears short skirts then she must be on drugs. Movies and television always make thoughtful parents look crazy, when I would actually say they are right. Those parents may not be able to explain their reasoning in an educated way, but they know that if they let their children live like the rest of the world, then they will fall prey to society's temptations. They're absolutely right about that. But it's difficult to raise your children well, because there is always the risk that they will rebel against any limitations you put in place. So, it's a difficult question.

The original question seemed to be about people who join cloistered religious societies. I know plenty of people who live and work in monasteries, and I know how monasteries are run—how they were organised historically and how they operate today. And I can tell you that joining a monastery or other closed society won't help you fix yourself. The people that are supposed to be living the cloistered life are already there. If you aren't already there, then that life isn't for you.

But if you're asking about unofficially walling yourself off from the world and being afraid of everything, then that won't help, either. It won't make you stronger in spirit or more aware or purer of heart. And you'll suffer financially, too. People joke about running off and joining a monastery or a convent to get away from temptation, but I think that's extreme. Wherever you go, there you are: the problems you have today will still be with you in a more restrictive environment. So, I would never advise anyone to take a radical step like that. All you need to do is live mindfully, exercise self-control, and keep from getting upset about the things you see in society. That's the best way to purify your soul, and it doesn't require you to take a vow of silence or anything else.

Question: Is it okay for me to tell someone I envy them?

Why would you do that? You won't change anything for the better, and the person you envy will be embarrassed or look down on you. I can't see anything positive coming from that conversation. If you realise that envy is something you struggle with, then talk about it, just not to the people you envy. Being open about your shortcomings is a good thing. Talk to your close friends. When you get together, instead of talking about some movie you watched or the new restaurant you just tried, talk about the things that worry you. Share what's in your heart. Tell them that you've realised that you have a lot of resentment or envy or whatever. Tell them what happened that made you feel small or unappreciated, and then listen to what they have to say. Maybe they'll share how they deal with the same issue. Or they'll laugh and show you how you're much bigger than whatever happened to you. Friends are such a strong driver of growth. But make sure that your friends are the kind of people who can make those deep dives with you. Stay away from people who only want to live on the surface. Make friends with people who are comfortable talking about their souls and about their feelings, people who will listen to you when you're worried. That dialogue and sharing has a healing effect.

Question: What about a family where the parents help one grown child more than the other? If the child who gets less help and attention is unhappy about it, would you call that envy?

Do you know what I dislike more than anything? People who are always offended. I've already shared what I think about people who resent their parents. And do you know where that mental junk comes from? It comes from people expecting others to provide for them instead of relying on themselves. That's a huge problem in society. People expect everything to be handed to them if they get good grades and go to college. That isn't how it works. You can't just expect your parents to give you everything you want, even if you come from a wealthy family. Don't go around counting other people's money. If your brother or sister or cousin does well for themselves, they don't owe you anything. And your parents don't owe you anything, either. They're just regular people. That's the first thing you have to understand: your relatives are just regular people. Don't go around comparing which of your family members are doing better financially and which of them are less well off. Comparisons will always make you unhappy. Two things are true: each of us is born in the family we deserve, and you are the only one who can change your life. You make the decisions that determine what happens to you.

If someone gives you money of their own free will, then that's wonderful. Be grateful and enjoy it. But don't sit around waiting for it to happen. If you want to be healthy, make choices that will improve your health. If you want a new car, save up and buy it. Don't hold your breath that someone is going to give it all to you. Everything is already in your hands. Go do the work that you know how to do and take care of your heart. The rest will follow.

I can't stand people who count every penny their parents give their siblings, who count all the birthday and Christmas gifts and add up what they're worth. When you resent your own family over those kinds of issues, the only person you're hurting is yourself.

Question: How can I avoid negative people and bad influences if you say they are everywhere?

Let me explain: if I read good books and socialise with good people, even online, if I do good deeds and keep my heart pure, then when I do go out in society, it's highly unlikely that I'll attract negative people or situations. I won't even notice them, and they'll do their best to avoid me. But let's say a negative person does end up close to you. Wherever you go in society, you will run into aggressive, angry people. There's nothing to worry about, though, because if you have a strong spirit and listen to your heart, that person won't be able to influence you. And you won't be bothered by them. That's how it works.

Question: Do feelings like resentment and envy exist on all the frequencies?

I wasn't planning to talk about frequencies just yet. First, not all of my readers are familiar with the idea. And second, I don't want to get distracted from the main topic. But I'll just say a few words about negative traits and frequencies to give you the general picture.

I do spend a fair amount of money on things like precious stones and artefacts because those are some of the things that help you turn off your negative energy and power up your positive traits. But don't think that you can just go out and buy some stones to improve your life without actually learning the other methods for personal growth. It doesn't work that way. If you don't understand how the human mind works and how we all suffer from negative traits and sin, then no stone or crystal can help you. So, forget about using frequencies as a shortcut to growth.

Question: When I see successful people with happy families on social media, it makes me want the same thing. Is that really so bad?

As long as you allow your attention and your time to be stolen by other people's images on social media, you will never have that success or that happy family. I can tell you that from personal experience. The more you stare at your phone, the less likely you are to be happy. That's not how happy people behave. But there's still hope if you realise what you're doing and take a step back from that social media-induced envy. Here's the secret to having a strong, happy family: stop thinking about it. Stop staring at other people's photographs. Better yet, get off social media altogether. That's the first step. The next step is to take care of your own life. Find people who vibe with you and do things that make your heart sing. When you stare at strangers' photos online, you're feeding them and neglecting your own life. That's a terrible cycle to get into. I tell people this all the time, but no one wants to listen. They get angry when I explain how it works. I've even been accused of envying the people who post all those happy family photos. The truth is, I just don't care about them. They can live however they want. My point is that you have to live your own life. The people who can't stop scrolling through social media and wishing that they had whatever it is that the influencers have—a bunch of kids, a good-looking spouse, whatever—are the people who do nothing to improve their own lives. If you're taking care of your own life, you don't have time to scroll through strangers' photos. It's that simple.

Question: I'm often afraid of offending certain people in my life. Is that okay, or should I get over it?

I'm tired of seeing people walk around in fear of doing the wrong thing or saying the wrong thing. From everything I've written so far, I would hope you understand that the people who are offended all the time are the ones who have the problems. Why should you always be afraid of offending someone? When I explain my understanding of how the mind works and how people can improve their lives, I speak openly without sugar coating anything. And if that offends someone, so be it. Because I understand how the system works, I do my best to bring that understanding to others. There's nothing wrong with that. It's the people who are mistaken and lead others into self-deception who will be punished by the system. My job is to speak the truth, to tear down deception and illusion. The truth isn't always sweet like sugar. But I always call a spade a spade. If you need to lose weight, I'll tell you. If you're lazy, I'll point it out. And I don't care if that makes people cry and get offended, because I'm not doing anything wrong. If you're living right and doing your best, I'll pat you on the back and say, "Good job! Carry on!"

There's no reason to keep the truth from people. If someone doesn't like it, then they need to work on themselves. It's ridiculous to tiptoe around out of fear that someone will be offended. I know many people would rather tell little lies and put up with people's nonsense and even make themselves sick rather than tell the truth and risk offending a relative or a neighbour. I understand that mindset, but my mission is to help people live a different way. Because keeping the peace at all costs just causes more suffering. The world doesn't work that way. In fact, it punishes people who will do anything to avoid rocking the boat.

It's hard to make people understand this, because fake politeness is so ingrained. But remember this: when you tell someone the truth, you give them a chance to grow. When you act like everything is fine, you deprive them of that chance. All because you're afraid they'll get offended. And meanwhile, the stress you hold inside can make you sick. So, don't be afraid to tell the truth.

Question: Alexandr, how do I get rid of my feelings of envy once and for all?

We will talk in greater detail about rooting out negative traits further on in the book. For now, we're just trying to understand how the negative characteristics reinforce each other and what causes them. But I'll give one idea to think about that may help you get rid of your problems on your own. The first method you should try is to identify the underlying cause. Before you can crush the negative trait, you have to crush the roots that feed it. It's a simple algorithm. Since you asked about envy, you would ask yourself, "What is causing my envy? What turns on that feeling in me?" Look at your social network feeds. Only follow people who aren't tempted by society's values. Now, you're wondering how to tell who those people are, right? Don't follow materialists. Stay away from boastful people. Those two pieces of advice alone should help you clean up your feed. Don't become a victim of social media show-offs. Don't waste your time on them. Follow real artists who are doing interesting work. Follow people who are inventing cool things or taking amazing photographs of puffins in Iceland. That's what your feed should be full of. Block anyone who posts negative political content or posts articles about terrible car accidents or kids getting hurt. Looking at content like that will attract misery into your life. I used to like Facebook, but it's so full of negative content now that I stay away. Even if it's your own friends or relatives posting that negative content, block them. And don't bother explaining your reasoning to them. They're already zombies. Just block anyone and everyone who posts negative, upsetting content.

Don't watch YouTube videos where people are unboxing stuff they buy or showing off new cars. That's all crap. And stay away from the angry, aggressive political commentators and the gossip channels where they tell you which billionaires are getting divorced. Stay away from all of it.

There is plenty of good content out there. I'm talking about the science channels, the art channels. Learn about black holes or watch bear cubs learning how to fish. Watch things that advance your understanding of the world. When you watch reality shows where they get people to yell at each other and threaten each other, you become part of that society. You may not always notice how what you watch affects you, but the effect is real. It controls your mood and your behaviour.

Forget about social media. If you have a friend who texts you all the time about how she got in a fight with her baby's daddy or flipped off someone on her way to work, block her. Surround yourself with positive, kind people that don't go around spreading negative thoughts. By doing so, you protect yourself not only from envy, but from all the other negative qualities like aggression and resentment.

Stay away from the YouTubers who promise to teach you how to succeed or how to open your own business. They make it look easy, and you feel like a loser if their system doesn't work for you. It's all filth and temptation.

You can also pay attention to the lighting in your house and the music you listen to, because those are important factors that affect your mood and your behaviour. I'll explain more about that later. For now, I just want to caution you about the content you're exposed to. Be careful what movies you watch. If you watch horror movies where people are getting their heads cut off, then don't be surprised when death stalks your family. Don't let yourself be entertained by death.

Question: Why do even very young children experience envy? Aren't they too young to be affected by society?

When I used to do readings of people's faces from photographs, one of my favourite questions was whether I could read children's faces. And it turned out that I can. See all the crap inside a person, no matter how old they are. Show me a photo of a three-year-old or a five-year-old, and if they're bad on the inside, I'll see it. I can see that a kid is going to get in trouble in school and grow up to beat his wife. I'm serious: I can see all of that in a photo of a small child. It's true that society influences us in negative ways, but don't forget about genetics. Children are born with a code that gives them their positive and negative traits. One child in a family might listen to their parents and understand why they're supposed to do certain things and not do other things, while that child's sibling—their twin, even—is born wanting to rebel and do everything their own way. They were simply born with different internal codes. The first one figured everything out in a previous life, and the second one didn't. Of course, life can turn certain character traits on and off, but that is secondary to the basic code. So, when I see children running around on the playground, I can tell who is evil and who isn't. It's an interesting paradox.

If you're a parent, you may have noticed this. When you take your child to the playground, you notice that some kids are kind and friendly while others run around shoving everyone. That's not the result of their upbringing. It's just who they are.

Getting back to the topic of how to get rid of your negative traits: people who have followed me for a long time remember that I used to offer a service that used frequencies to help people get rid of their negative characteristics. Good, kind people vibrate on one frequency, while people who are mean and angry vibrate on a different frequency. Your frequency determines your mood and your thoughts. When I explained this, people started signing up for me to help them get onto new frequencies so they could get rid of their negative traits.

One person asked me to create a frequency for him that would clear him of all his negative energy, because he was feeling angry and upset all the time. Always losing his temper with people. So, I created a frequency called *Peace*. When it worked, I built a workshop around it and started selling it. It's made up of elements that feed your soul and starve the demon inside you. They starve your shortcomings and sins. When you're living on the *Peace* frequency, all your desires go away: sexual desires, the desire to lie and hurt people and get angry. All of it goes away.

That's just one way to work out your negative traits. I want you to know about the options so you have hope for your future, but for right now, let's keep focusing on noticing these traits in ourselves, on where we should be focusing our attention. We've talked about pride and envy and even a little bit about resentment. Now that we've covered envy, you should have a better understanding of the people around you who are affected by it. You should know it when you see it. And you should have a better sense of your own envy and what activates it. Once we've looked at all the different sins, it will be time to talk in detail about getting rid of them.

Anger

The next sin we will talk about is anger. I don't want you to be confused by false information, so before you go online to read about what anger is, I'd appreciate it if you would first write out your own thoughts on the topic. I'm much more interested in your ideas than in something you read on the internet. So, look inside yourself and see how you're put together. See how you understand the word anger and write it down in a notebook.

Now that you're back, I'll tell you how I understand anger, and I'll keep it simple. Anger is an aggressive reaction to something. Like pride and resentment, it's a feeling that overwhelms you. Because I'm an empath, I can smell a person's anger when I walk in the room, even if I have no idea what's been going on.

It's difficult to be around angry people. You've probably had this experience: you're riding in a car and your friend is driving. He's just minding his own business, maybe the two of you are talking about something. But then another car cuts him off, and suddenly your friend is furious. So, angry that you're scared of what he'll do. It's a reaction that comes from deep inside.

I've spent thirty years studying people and their reactions, and I can tell you that different people have different levels of anger. I've met plenty of people who seemed fine on the outside, but if something didn't go their way, they would get angry. Paradoxically, though, not every person is prone to anger. The only people who get angry in a situation are the ones who have that anger inside. For some people, their anger is a tiny flame. For others, it's like a giant balloon that swells up inside them. You may not always be aware of the anger in the people around you. Maybe someone in your life gets angry once every few years, or maybe they lose their temper every few hours over tiny things like traffic or bad service in a restaurant.

Anger hurts the people around you. I can't be near angry people. I literally ran away from them. Think about all the times you've met someone who seems nice enough, but as soon as they drop their cell phone or some other minor annoyance happens, they get so angry that they look like they could kill someone.

Anger also increases over time. The more often a person is angry, the more rage they have inside them. Like all the other sins and negative traits, anger is interconnected, usually with resentment. When someone stores up a lot of resentment, eventually it ferments and turns into anger.

Here's an interesting paradox: half of the people who know me would tell you that I'm incredibly kind, and the other half would tell you that I'm incredibly angry. Why is that? Well, there's a difference between speaking harshly to someone and being angry. I can be tough on someone and raise my voice without feeling anger or anything else negative inside. Sensitive people know the difference. There's a big difference between being tough and being angry. Anger is an instinctual reaction that makes you feel sick because you're essentially rotting inside. You can't control it.

When I come down hard on someone to get their attention, I'm like an actor. I'm in control. I may frown and raise my voice, I may even use some choice words, but it isn't anger. You need to understand the difference. Some people live on a frequency where they can't hear you unless they think you're angry with them, so that's why I have to speak harshly. But I'm not angry.

The sin we call anger is an aggressive reaction to something you don't like or can't control. You may be the nicest person most of the time, but if you allow yourself to be controlled by anger, then you become a source of evil for the people around you. Ninety-nine per cent of people allow anger to control them at least some of the time. The people I hire for my projects are wonderful for the most part, but almost all of them have some negative traits, and anger is usually right there at the top of the list.

Since I'm single, people sometimes ask me what kind of woman I would be interested in. I always say that my number one criterion is that she not be angry.

Angry people are demons. The person I live with has to be kind all the way through, without a single ounce of anger.

Remember: when you are maximally pure, you can't get angry. It's impossible. Something may shock you or make you cry, but you won't feel angry. I already mentioned that anger borders on resentment, but it also borders fear. All those things live together and rot you from the inside out.

Keep in mind that a person can be strict with themselves and others without being angry. A leader who makes their team work hard and demands accountability is not necessarily displaying anger. The difference is in their feelings. Accountability is calm and cool. It's a necessity. Anger is an animal instinct that you can't control.

Questions and Answer about Anger

Question: Is it anger if a person is easily annoyed and loses their temper?

I believe so. I haven't read books about this; I just tell you what I perceive with my senses. When a person gets annoyed all the time, they are full of angry energy. It's the same code inside, even if the causes are different.

That kind of behaviour is infectious, like a virus. Imagine that an angry person says something awful about your mother or father. How do you feel? Your first reaction is pain, like someone stabbed you in the heart. Then you get angry, too. You want to strike back at that person. That kind of uncontrolled, aggressive reaction is anger, too.

If you're pure inside, you won't react that way no matter what someone says to you. Does that mean you won't stick up for your mother or father? Of course not. You will defend the person being criticised unfairly, but you'll do it with love in your heart. Do you see the difference? Turning away from anger does not mean letting people walk all over you. It just means controlling your emotions and acting out of love.

Question: I had a falling-out with an old friend several years ago. He says he isn't angry at me anymore, but whenever we hang out, I feel his resentment. What can I do about it? I want to save this friendship.

I used to think of this kind of situation as a knot that needed to be untied. I wanted to help people who were stuck with resentment, stuck with unresolved problems. But then I grew up and saw more of the world and realised that I would be wasting my time. In your case, you're wasting your time worrying about your friend.

Why do I say that? It's not because I don't care. I speak and write books because I want people to grow and get free of whatever is holding them back. So, I definitely care. But you have to understand your place in life. Everyone you meet is at their own level of personal growth. Think of it like a game: if you're at level four and your friend is at level one, there's not much you can do for him. If he didn't have that resentment against you, I guarantee you he would be hating on someone else. Even if the two of you had never met and never had that falling-out, he would be pissed off about something.

It's a big world with a lot of people in it. When you change yourself, all of a sudden you are surrounded by people at your same level. So, don't waste your time on someone who isn't ready to change. You can't help your friend, and you'll only make yourself unhappy.

You may be reading this and thinking that it sounds harsh. Friends are supposed to stick together through thick and thin, right? Nope. Those old-school values don't work anymore. Maybe they never did. Everything in your life that you aren't satisfied with—your negative traits, how much money you make, even your mood—is a function of the people around you. But strangely, when people are dissatisfied with their lives, they turn their backs on God. "Everything in my life is going wrong, so there must be no God." Or they get angry at the government. Both of those reactions are really common.

Here's the truth: your problems have nothing to do with God or the government. It's all the people you keep around you.

The people in your life have an enormous influence on you. That's why you should stay away from that old friend who acts like he's mad at you and doesn't want to talk about it. Why should you marinate in his negative energy? He's already being punished by having to live a life full of resentment, and it's his job to figure it out. It's his burden, his sin. So, let go. Put your own life in order and spend your time around healthy, positive people.

I divided this book into two volumes, sins and virtues, for a good reason: I want us to get through the dark material about sin and then move on to the better stuff. It's like a physical pathway. We pass through the dark forest and then come out in the light. We stir up the anthill and look at what comes out, and then we turn our attention to something happier. Do the same with your friend. Understand where he's at, and then move on so you can spend your energy on building up your own positive traits. Spend time with people who really love you.

Questions: Where does anger come from?

This is an important question, and it's something I feel strongly about. I used to be in a relationship with a woman who suffered from resentment and anger that seemed to be triggered by everyone and everything, and I felt all those emotions like they were my own. Meditation helped, but it was still painful. That experience informs how I think about anger.

In my professional life, I'd rather hire someone who has a lot to learn than a terrific expert who has anger inside. My team is made up of extremely sensitive, kind people, and if a new hire turns out to be angry, the rest of the team gets upset. They can't stop worrying about that person. We try to avoid problems by being careful about who we hire, but if we have to, we would rather let someone go than stew in their anger all day.

But let's return to your question, which was about where anger comes from. I want to share what happened to a good friend of mine, because it perfectly illustrates how anger moves through groups of people like a virus. I had a close friend who was one of the nicest, most laid-back people you ever met. No matter what the people around him did or said, he never got angry. It was like he didn't know how. But then he moved away, and I didn't see him for five years. When he moved back and we started spending time together again, I started noticing signs of anger in him. He'd be fine for a day or two, and then something would set him off and he turned negative really fast. As you can imagine, I was in shock. Naturally, I tried to figure out what had happened. Because that's what I do professionally, and because this was a close friend. What I discovered was this: my friend was in a relationship with a woman who was controlled by anger, and she had unwittingly tuned him to her frequency. Neither one of them meant for that to happen. When you spend a lot of time around an angry person, you start to pick up on that anger and experience it like it's your own. My friend's girlfriend was also frequently irritated with him, and that eventually made him respond in anger.

From the messages that people send me, I know that a lot of you struggle with your loved ones' anger. It's scary at first, and that's a normal reaction. But then you start to get angry, too. And if you're the one who struggles with anger, it helps if you understand that you picked it up from someone else. Someone gave it to you. It might have been a relative or an intimate partner, or it may have been someone at work. Sadly, some people pick up their anger from their parents in childhood.

My advice is this: no matter what, don't let yourself fall into the anger trap. If your relative or friend or colleague keeps trying to make you match their anger, don't play the game. As soon as you play the game, you've lost. In my own life, I will go to extremes to avoid conflict with people. For example, if I'm at a party and someone makes fun of me or tries to bait me into arguing with them, I won't respond in anger. Instead, I'll say, "Sure, you're welcome to think I'm an idiot. You're welcome to say it out loud. If you want, I'll even get down on my knees and admit it. Would you like that?" They may think I'm crazy, but I'd rather put a stop to the conversation that way than get worked up trying to prove myself to someone who doesn't like me. I'd rather pay for their drinks than argue with them.

It's always better to cry about something than to get mad about it. If you feel yourself starting to get angry, don't feed it. Avoid the person or the situation that gives rise to those feelings in you. If you always end up yelling at your family when you sit down to do your taxes, hire an accountant. If going to the home improvement store makes you a ball of rage, just order what you need online and pay extra for delivery. Take care of yourself whenever and however you can. Don't watch violent films or listen to violent music. Stay away from aggressive entertainment in general. And don't forget to create a community of kind, loving people around you so that you can boost your positive traits while you avoid feeding your anger.

Question: I'm good at controlling my anger. Does that still mean that I have a problem? Is it possible to have so little anger inside that it doesn't matter?

Let me say this again: anger is what you feel *inside*. If you are furious and out of control inside, it doesn't matter how skilled you are at not showing it. That's anger and it's a negative force in your life. With true self-control, you aren't angry inside. You may use your tone of voice and your facial expression to show dissatisfaction, but inside you are calm and collected.

Now, for the second part of the question: any amount of anger acts like a poison. It's harder to rile a person with less anger, but it's still possible. Someone like that might fly off the handle every month or so, maybe even less, and only in serious situations. But a person who has a lot of anger—imagine that they're blown up like a balloon full of rage—is going to be provoked by something every day. They'll scream at you for the tiniest thing. Even standing next to someone like that is frightening.

So, I never said that it's okay to have a little bit of anger if you can control it. Any amount of anger is going to cause trouble in your life and your relationships. What I meant when I said that some people have very little anger is that you might not notice it, at least not right away. You might see someone every day for a month and only see one episode of rage. There are different levels of anger, but it's all the same problem.

Question: Can you talk about how hormones control our moods?

That's a different language. I'm not a doctor, and I don't use medical terms. All that talk of serotonin and dopamine and oestrogen and testosterone just confuses people, in my opinion. The people who use those words live on the surface of our existence, and they often use them without understanding what they really mean. When I meet individuals, who want to converse with me in those terms—or better yet, using words like perfectionist, optimist, pessimist, introvert, and extrovert—I'm out. I tell them, "You don't understand yourself, so you make things complicated with all these terms." I'd rather keep it simple and achieve true understanding than go digging into the medical and psychological terminology. There's no need to consult a doctor to understand your own mind. The value of what I teach is that I use the simplest words and the simplest examples so that absolutely anyone can understand. I get right at the heart of the problem.

You asked about hormones and how they affect us. Let's talk about that in the simplest terms possible. A person's mood can change for a variety of reasons. Women have a couple of days every month where their mood suffers. But look at a woman who is free from anger and aggression. When it's her time of the month, she might be more sensitive and more emotional, but she won't be angry.

Don't confuse anger and sensitivity. Those big feelings will be there, but they won't have anything to do with anger. The women who experience a lot of rage every month are the ones who already had that rage inside of them.

Hunger is another factor that can affect a person's mood. The first time I heard someone say they were 'hangry' I didn't get it. That's not how my body works. But I've seen it enough times now to recognise it: there's this irritability that hits people when they're hungry, and once they eat it goes away. Here's the thing, though. That irritability has nothing to do with food. Your friend or family member is getting angry because they have anger inside. Hunger provokes it, and food pacifies it. It's a strange thing, but it's a good example of how we may not only notice anger in people because it only comes out in certain situations.

Question: I've heard religious people say that we just have to learn to harness our anger for a good purpose. What do you think about that?

Use your anger for good. I've heard that one in at least a dozen sports movies. It sounds nice, but it's easier said than done. Do those same religious people have any advice for getting rid of anger so it doesn't control your life? No, they don't. Instead, they tell you to use your anger as an alternative fuel source. Tame it and use it. Become a champion boxer, right?

But that's not how it works. You can play every sport in the Olympics and still be eaten up inside with anger. I'm fairly sure that if you ask someone living a serious religious life what they mean when they say 'use your anger for good,' they'd break it down like I just did. They'd explain that they want you to use up that anger getting things done, accomplishing something positive. And if you asked them how to actually *get rid* of that anger instead of just redirecting it, they'd tell you to meditate. At least that's what a Buddhist monk would say.

Question: If my partner is an angry person, does that mean there's no way I can avoid becoming angry, too?

As I explained before, when you live with an angry person, you catch their anger. There are a few exceptions, though, and it all depends on how strong you are and how pure your heart is. If you're strong and spiritual, you can live with a demon and not be destroyed. You may be damaged, but you'll hold up. If there's any weakness in you, though, the anger and aggression will seep in.

The other exception to that rule are all the people who live on a frequency where they don't feel other people's emotions. I live on a spiritual frequency where I can feel people's energy, but there are people who don't pick up on that information. They see their loved ones' faces and hear their words, but they don't pick up on their feelings. If a person smiles at them or compliments them, they react favourably because they aren't receiving any information about that person's energy.

People who don't pick up on the feelings of those around them can live with an angry partner and not be affected by it. They can work at jobs where they're surrounded by negativity. Their secret is being closed off.

I used to advise people to try to close themselves off to protect themselves from negative family members or friends. If you don't want to pick up your relative's negative energy, stop being so sensitive. There was a time when I would have said that. But times have changed. You can't wall yourself off from other people anymore. It's important to let your flame be seen, to live by your heart. It's important to be sensitive, if that's what you are. The more often you listen to your own inner voice, the better. Keeping a diary is a great way to do this.

Materialists react strangely when I tell them there are cities I just can't live in. They say, "But those are all beautiful cities with good restaurants and great architecture!" My answer is this: none of that matters when the people in a city all give off negative energy. The people who are capable of feeling it understand me, but the people who don't notice think I've lost my mind. They like their cities just fine, and here I come telling them that the people there smell like death to me. I can sense the crime, the aggression, and the anger in people. There are good people everywhere you go, of course, but I stay away from cities where the majority of people are angry. So, you see, I don't choose where to live based on restaurants and architecture, because those are shallow things. I choose based on the quality of the people.

It's important to be able to see past the surface and understand who people really are. You asked if it's possible to live with a negative, angry person. Here's my answer: you have to commit to a lot of personal growth before you can choose that path. You're going to feel the effects of that anger, or you're going to have to wall yourself off from it.

I expect that your next question is "Can I help my significant other with their anger?" No, you can't. They have to help themselves, and you have to take care of yourself. There is no way for you to work with them directly on that anger. But here's another thought: if you have a strong heart, then that negativity won't drag you down. If you work on becoming as pure as possible, your loved one's anger won't affect you, and your kindness could even drown out some of that anger. Does that motivate you to work on yourself? The stronger your spirit, the greater the chance that you will avoid the negative effects of your partner's anger and maybe have a beneficial effect on them. But they have to be willing to do the work themselves.

Question: Will my anger go away if I avoid the situations that provoke me and surround myself with goodness and light?

That's exactly how it works. This book is a quest of sorts, because I use examples and even digressions to give you a break and let you absorb the lessons without thinking about it too much. You've done a great job with that quest! I haven't really shared much with you yet about getting rid of the negative qualities, but we're getting to it. Everything will be in the right time. I don't want to distract you from our main goal, which is to gain a deeper understanding. I want to break the seals for you so you see the dark side of the human heart. And I use examples instead of big words so that when you see negative traits in a person, you'll get it right away, and you'll be careful around them. You'll understand that, while the person isn't necessarily bad, they have these bad traits that cause problems. And you'll understand how easy it is to slip and become an angry, negative person. Some of you have probably started to realise that you don't have the negative traits you were worried about.

Question: Are there any techniques for dealing with anger that really work? How can I calm myself down when I get upset? Do the methods they show in the movie 'Anger Management' really work?

I remember the movie 'Anger Management' with Adam Sandler. His character was a nice guy, he just couldn't control his temper. And the movie shows all these different ways to achieve self-control. But that's not really how it works. But you're getting ahead of yourself. Or at least you're getting ahead of me. I never recommend turning to movies for advice on how to live your life, anyway.

The experience I'm drawing from in this book is my own personal experience, not movies or books or other people's stories. I first encountered society—the world of other people—when I was twenty-five or thereabouts. I was like a fluffy little kitten that left home for the first time. For a while, I learned and talked to wise people and wrote books, but then I got sucked into society. That's when I found out about frequencies: you vibrate along with the people around you. They affect your mood, your thoughts, everything. I wasn't very aware, I wasn't on the path yet, so I did like everyone around me and tuned in to a frequency.

Every week or so, I'd make an attempt to get off that frequency. I'd write a chapter in my book or record a video or hold a workshop. And then I'd get sucked into social life again, where I was overwhelmed by other people's emotions. It was shocking. I had never realised how other people felt before. I tried all the frequencies and picked up all the negative traits that we're talking about. I got myself in, and then I got myself out. I know where negative traits come from and how to get rid of them.

I also have years of personal experience helping my clients root out the negative traits that keep them from living their true lives. There are five methods I'm going to share with you for starving the anger and the envy and all the rest of it, but first you have to understand where they come from. You can't treat the disease until you know what it's like to be healthy. You have to at least understand that basic fact first. None of the methods I'm going to give you will work without an understanding of how our hearts work, and that's what I'm giving you right now. I'm showing you how we're made. This is the information you need to master before you can truly control yourself, turning off your negative traits and turning up your positive ones. The key is understanding.

So, don't try to jump ahead and think of ways to control yourself just yet, especially if you're getting your inspiration from movies. Stick with me and you'll get there.

Question: If a person only listens to you when you yell at them, does that mean that they have anger in them, too?

Not necessarily. Some people are absent-minded. Or busy. Or shy. Or they were raised by someone who yelled at them all the time and they don't know any other way of being. For the college students out there, maybe you have a roommate who's really forgetful. You tell them, "Hey, don't forget to set your alarm. You have a big exam in the morning, remember?" No reaction. Then you remind them again before you go to sleep, and you use a polite tone of voice because that's how you're accustomed to treating people. But they don't hear you. They forget to set the alarm and sleep through the test. Infuriating, right?

What if you had tried a different tactic? Maybe you grabbed your roommate by the shoulder and said, "Look me in the eye. I want you to march over to your bedside table and set your alarm right now. And I'm going to watch you do it. If you miss that test tomorrow, I'll rip you a new one." I bet your roommate would have straightened up and paid attention. They would set the alarm, go to bed, and be on time for the exam. That's how some people are. They don't hear you when you talk to them politely, but when you yell at them, they pay attention.

But does that mean they're angry people at heart? No, it doesn't. A lot of them are just absent-minded and foolish.

Question: I have a really strange reaction when people get angry at me: I start to laugh. Have you ever heard that before?

Sure, lots of people laugh at what we would consider the wrong time. Some people laugh when they're scared or upset. Others laugh when someone yells at them. It's a defensive mask. A way of protecting yourself. Most of the time, I don't see anything wrong with it. It's better to laugh and smile than to get angry in response.

Here's the drawback: laughing when someone is angry at you will just make them madder. Why is that? Because when a person is mad at you, they want you to be scared. They want you to give up. And here you are laughing. That's just going to make them even angrier.

Let's say your shower overflows and gets my bathroom ceiling wet. And this isn't the first time it's happened. So, I come upstairs and start shouting at you. If you lean against the doorframe and start laughing in my face, I might be tempted to knock your head off. (This is all hypothetical, of course.) Instead of admitting fault and apologising to show that you care about me, you're laughing like a hyena. Obviously, that's not going to sit well with me.

Question: I was always a calm, happy person until I had a baby. Now, I feel so angry sometimes that I just can't control myself.

I've heard about this happening so many times. Women are naturally upset when they realise that their own child provokes them to anger. There's nothing wrong with you or your child—that's one thing you can stop worrying about.

In simple terms, your nervous system is weak right now. There are a lot of factors involved, from hormones to food and vitamins to sleep. Without getting into a medical discussion, any time you aren't getting enough sleep, aren't eating enough, and don't have time to rest, your nervous system is going to suffer. Those are things to talk to a doctor about. But in simple terms, I'd just say that you're exhausted, and that makes you feel irritated more than you normally would. Your spirit is weak and worn down because you aren't taking care of yourself, and that puts you at the mercy of your big feelings.

When young people who don't have children yet come to me for help dealing with anger, I tell them to get a dog. Raising a puppy is a great opportunity to learn about yourself. Say the puppy chews up your favourite shoes or poops on your carpet. That's a quick way to find out what kind of things provoke your anger. If you pay attention and watch yourself interact with your puppy, choosing kindness and patience over anger, you'll be much better prepared to handle other people, including a baby. When a colleague at work messes something up or your toddler knocks a lamp off the table and breaks it, you realize that the only thing you can control is your own reaction. You're the one in charge of that.

In that sense, children raise us—not the other way around. They give us a chance to really see ourselves in action. That's growth, my friends. Becoming an emotionally stable parent means taking care of yourself, taking breaks, and surrounding yourself with positive people. And once you're stable, your child won't be able to provoke you anymore.

Question: Can I become a better person by letting my anger out?

This is something people ask about a lot. I've already explained that anger starts inside you. It's a reaction that happens inside, whether or not you show it. But I'll go further and say that once you're angry, it's better to let it out than to try to hide it. Holding in feelings like anger can destroy you over a period of years. It happens slowly, and people are often surprised when they realise that the problems in their life have grown along with their anger.

Don't think that letting your anger out will cure it, though. You're just letting off steam. When you bottle up your anger inside, it starts to turn into resentment or even a desire for revenge against the person who angered you. It can even turn into hate. See how the list just goes on? All these negative traits reinforce each other.

And there are other things to consider. When you blow off steam, you scare people. And you make them angry right along with you. So, while you may relieve your own stress, you pass that stress to other people. Spreading aggression is never a good idea. If you get angry enough and show it, you could end up doing something you'll regret for the rest of your life. You could even get arrested.

So, if you're risking your health when you keep your anger inside and risking your relationships and your future when you let it out, what can you do? I'll say it again: keep a diary. Or find someone who will listen to you before you get so angry that you feel like exploding. But it's important to always ask that person's permission. Don't pour your pent-up rage out on someone who hasn't consented to listen.

That's an interesting issue that comes up with anger. People are smart, and they have instincts for self-preservation. So, when your boss comes down on you unfairly, you don't show your anger. You keep it hidden. When your co-worker tries to get you in trouble, you keep your cool. But once you're home, around your family where you feel more comfortable, you start to let it out. Even though your family has nothing to do with the underlying cause of your feelings.

I've had people use me that way, like a trash can where they can dump their crap. I don't like it, but I understand that it has nothing to do with me. If it's a friend of mine, I know that he held it in at work, and he held it in at home around his kids, and when it was just the two of us, he couldn't hold it in anymore. Any time, someone holds their anger in for a long time, they eventually let it loose on the first person they think won't retaliate or won't care. It's almost like a game: the anger gets handed around from one person to the next, and everyone's afraid it will explode on them. But again, if it's a friend, I won't respond by blowing up on him. I understand that he couldn't hold it in anymore.

And yet, screaming at people is never okay. It hurts people, and you can't go back and undo the damage. So, don't let yourself get to the point that you lose control. What I suggest instead is that you rely on rituals to keep yourself balanced emotionally. Does that sound mystical? In fact, most religions have some kind of ritual. You could take this literally and go to confession at church. Or as an alternative, you could keep a diary—on paper or as short videos—where you work through your pain and let your anger out. If you have a close friend who agrees to listen, make time to talk with them regularly. Go out for a beer or a glass of wine and tell them about everything that made you angry that week. You'll feel unburdened, and you won't be as likely to lose control and yell at someone.

I'll be honest with you here: there are some solid short-term solutions in that last paragraph, but I'm not entirely satisfied with the answer because I don't like the question. It assumes that you only have two choices: holding your anger in or letting it out. And that just isn't true. I'm not here to teach you how to cope with anger. I want you to live free from anger. And the real way to deal with anger is to dig in and figure out what's causing it. You have to find the cause and do something about it. Once you do that, your aggression will be gone, like magic.

Question: Is there ever anything positive about anger and aggression?

I've already mentioned how a person's negative traits can push them to work hard and achieve a lot. And I explained how despite all that hard work, the person is still on the wrong frequency. It's always better to work hard and achieve your goals because of the kindness and love you have inside. When you recognise your negative trait and keep using it to fuel your own advancement, you've essentially made a bargain with the devil where you agree to keep living with that negative trait. Something happened to you earlier in life and turned you into an angry person, and now you want to know if you can use that aggression for gain.

Sure, I suppose you can, but how? By scaring people, for starters. If you have a conflict and the other person is mad at you, you can raise your voice and make your eyes bulge out to show that you're ten times madder. Or a hundred times. However much you want. The other person will probably back down, and you'll feel like a winner. But you aren't: you're just feeding your own anger and provoking the other person to anger. And you're showing that you only have that one tool for dealing with people.

Instead, you should try to find a positive, more productive way to deal with people, even the ones you have conflicts with. Take the high road whenever you can.

Question: Are you saying I shouldn't feel angry when I step on a nail? How is that even possible?

I'll explain it again: when you have crap inside you, that crap is going to come out sometimes. When you're surprised, when you hit your thumb with a hammer, when you scratch the finish on your car against a concrete pole. Any of a hundred things will provoke you to anger.

But if you're emotionally stable and have a pure heart, you won't lose your temper when you scratch your car. You won't even get mad when someone else scratches your car. Because the crap just isn't there. If you step on a nail, you'll be in pain for sure, but you won't be angry.

People who are full of anger lose their tempers over anything: they spilled their coffee, the red light took too long to change, the person in front of them at the grocery store wasn't moving fast enough. Any little thing can make them crazy and spoil their day. That's how unstable they are. That's a terrible way to live. So, here's my answer: the nail is just a provocation. The reaction comes from inside you. If you're pure inside and don't harbour anger, then you won't be hopping around mad, cursing up a blue streak. Instead, you clean up your foot, put a bandage on it, and look up the date of your last tetanus booster. Inside, your heart feels just as light as it did before you stepped on the nail. The problem isn't the nail, or the neighbour who dinged your car, or the dog that chewed up your brand-new kicks. The problem is you.

Question: If I'm angry all the time because I'm disappointed in myself, then I guess the only way to get rid of the anger is to meet my own expectations. Or should I lower those expectations to make it easier to get rid of the anger?

What does it mean to be disappointed in yourself? For most people, it means wishing you looked a certain way or wishing you could buy certain things. You think that if you could improve your appearance or buy those things, your disappointment in yourself and the anger it fuels would go away. But here's the catch: your anger sits much deeper than any of those shallow concerns. They just provoke it; they aren't the true source. The longer you let that anger fester, however, the more likely it is that other things will start to provoke it, too. That's how it works.

Instead of worrying about your expectations, you need to work on your frequency and your heart. Clean out your heart and get rid of your anger. Then focus on accepting yourself the way you are. After that, you won't feel so negative about yourself. So, first you have to clean out your heart and get rid of your anger. Taking away the thing that angers you is just a temporary fix. If the trash can under my desk annoys me because the lid doesn't close right, I can get rid of it and buy a nicer one. If I can't stand my neighbour or his dog, I can go inside whenever I see them coming. But I'll still be the kind of person who gets annoyed by little things. I haven't done anything to really help myself. You can go around your house and get rid of all the things—and people—that bother you, and you'll feel better. But only for a while. Everyone tries this. It's called running away from yourself. You're pointing your finger at everything that annoys you without looking into your own soul and your own mind. If anything, running away from yourself eventually makes you feel worse, because you have to remove more and more things (and people!).

I've always taken the opposite approach. I look at the things that bother me, but I don't remove them from my life. Instead, I work on becoming stronger so that I'm not as easily annoyed. Try meditation and other techniques until you find one that works for you. Keep working until you don't experience that old annoyance anymore. The nice thing about this approach is that it makes you so much freer as you move through the world. Then you don't have to hide from things. That's real growth.

Question: You said that some people are born with negative traits. Can you do anything about traits you're born with?

This question brings us straight to the meaning of life. In some of my other books and videos, I've talked about how your soul is a mosaic made up of lots of tiny pieces. Some of those pieces are good ones, others are bad. And the whole meaning of life is to take the weaknesses you're born with and turn them into something better. You weren't born to fail because of those weaknesses. You were born to do something about them. That's what growth is all about.

We humans may be born on different continents, with different colours of skin and hair, with different religions, different genders, but all of us fall prey to illusion. We fight, we harbour resentment against each other, fall in love with each other, betray each other, but it's all an illusion. The whole reason we are alive is so that we can find and air out our negative traits and feed and encourage our positive traits. That's our life's work.

Question: I feel bad when I don't achieve my goal or when I lose at a game. Is that anger?

Feeling sad when you lose or when you don't get something you worked for is different from reacting with anger. Those are two very different things. If what you're experiencing ranges from irritation all the way to rage—whether at yourself or at someone else—then that is exactly the sin we are talking about. But if you're sad or disappointed, that's something else. Sometimes, there's a fine line, so pay attention to those feelings. Try to identify them. And remember, your anger is harmful even if you control yourself. You don't have to whack your opponent over the head with the game board to have an anger problem. Just feeling anger inside is enough to hurt you and those around you.

Question: Are you saying that if my significant other leaves me and breaks my heart, then the pain I feel is my own problem?

That's exactly what I'm saying. You were walking around imagining you had the perfect partner, and then you were disillusioned all of a sudden and that hurts. But get this: when you thought everything was wonderful, you were living an illusion. Your partner never belonged to you. They have their own path and their own personality traits that complicate things. They have to figure life out just like everybody else, and they make mistakes, just like you.

When you feel anger and resentment toward them because they left you, that's on you. You assumed that you owned your partner, but you don't. I've had people start to think that they own a piece of me just because I helped them out with their careers or gave them money when they were broke. See how that works? All I did was help someone, and in their mind I belong to them. They don't understand that I wasn't trying to buy their friendship or make myself look important. I just saw someone who needed help and did what I could. Once they were on their feet again, I moved along. Some people are hurt by that, and some get angry.

So, learn to look at people as separate from yourself. Never forget that you don't own the people around you.

Question: Can you explain what you meant when you said that anger borders on fear?

Absolutely. That's one of the first things I noticed when I started partying with one-percenters. They had bodyguards and huge bank accounts and connections with important people, but they were all scared of something, while I wasn't. And they noticed the difference. I think anger is the connection.

When you're a believer—and you don't just believe in your own mind—then you accept yourself and your life the way it is. You don't have anything to hide. You don't have skeletons in the closet that you have to keep people from finding out about. When something frightening or unexpected happens, you aren't afraid. If someone robbed me at gunpoint, I wouldn't be afraid. I'd give them my phone and my wallet, and then I'd think, "Let's see what happens next." That's my approach to life. I wait to see what's going to happen next, and I try to understand why God put me in that situation. It's all about acceptance.

Most of the people around you are full of fear because they aren't sure of themselves and don't believe in anything outside of themselves. And all that fear makes them angry. It's a defensive reaction. When people feel weak and defenceless, they react in anger. If you aren't afraid of anything, then logically you have no reason to react aggressively. When someone threatens you, more likely than not you've just done something that made them afraid of you. As long as you don't pour oil on their flames, they aren't dangerous to you; they think you are dangerous to them.

When someone displays anger at you, the best thing you can do is not react at all. They're trying to pull you down to their level. They expect you to be on the same frequency. And if you remain calm, they won't know what to do.

Over the years, there have been people who have tried to hurt me by damaging my online presence. They set up fake accounts to write negative comments on my posts and think that somehow they're hurting me. I think they expect me to get mad and argue with them or try to get their accounts banned. But I never react. They don't understand that at my scale, their comments can't hurt me, especially if I don't pay any attention to them. I create the content I want to create, and if someone doesn't like it, that's on them. Go ahead and send me death threats: nothing scares me. That's what I want for each of you—to live your life without fear.

Question: How do I figure out if a person has anger inside before I meet them?

Do you mean before you physically come into contact with them? That's hard to do. Even I can't do it all the time. If a person's heart is made up of less than 10% anger, you won't be able to tell just by looking at a photograph. If they have more than 10% anger, though, you can see it. They may only lose their temper once a year, but I'll be able to see it in a photograph. It's in their eyes.

My friends used to drive me crazy showing me photos of people all the time and wanting me to tell them everything I saw. It wasn't always because they wanted to gain valuable information, either. I think they wanted to see if I would ever make a mistake. That's a shame, because the information is worthwhile. As an example, I looked at a photo of the head of a well-known design studio and was able to describe him in detail. And that's without reading any of his interviews for hints about his personality. It was all in his face. I saw his face and could say with certainty that he's a negative person, full of anger, resentment, envy, greed. All of it together. He may be the best designer out there, but you wouldn't want to be his partner.

I want to point out here that just because a person is full of anger or envy doesn't mean they aren't great at what they do. There's a musician I have tons of respect for whose face shows extreme levels of anger and resentment. His music is his own; he never borrows anything from anyone else. But when I look at him, I can tell that his personal life is full of conflict. I listen to his music, but I would never advise someone to be in a relationship with him or do business with him. Those are different things.

I see a lot of negative people in the media. Journalists like to stir up trouble and make people angry. If you call them out on it, they say they're trying to help their communities. But if you watch them, they never actually do anything useful. They write clickbait stories about how the government ought to do this or that or the other because that's what gets the ratings. It's all about getting ads in front of eyeballs. They never lift a finger to actually make their communities work better. Do you see the contradiction there? Don't be fooled by negative people who use their forked tongues to distort how you see the world around you.

But life is hope. All those negative traits and negative actions are just unfinished projects. Life is all about taking those unfinished projects and growing so you can turn them into something good. There's nothing wrong with that. All of us change during our lives, so there's always hope for the egotistical, the angry, the envious among us. They can change. Their negative characteristics can die out, and their positive characteristics can grow stronger. Each of us has our own path. So, even though I sometimes call these negative traits sins, that doesn't mean I believe people are doomed. There's no such thing as a 'bad' person. If we found ourselves in other people's shoes, we'd probably behave just like they do. I hope that you'll keep that in mind when we get to our discussion of positive characteristics, because understanding and empathy are always the best tools for dealing with difficult people. Whether or not you saw them coming.

Question: My 14-year-old daughter is always angry at her mom. What can I do to help this situation?

This is one of the most frequent questions I get asked. Since I don't have children, it rubs some people the wrong way that I even venture an answer. But interestingly, the instincts I had years ago when I was still a student have held up well. So, no, I don't have children, but the understanding I can give you isn't specific to children, anyway.

I wouldn't worry too much about your daughter, if I were you. Around age 12—sometimes earlier, sometimes later—80% of girls start spending more time in their rooms and less time talking to their parents. The other 20% don't seem to have that problem, but they're in the minority. So, your daughter is absolutely normal in that respect. Talk to other parents of teenage daughters and you'll see what I mean. At this age, girls are more influenced by society than boys, and they also have to deal with mood swings and other aspects of growing up. Women are generally more susceptible to social influences than men are, so it makes sense that girls would show the same signs.

But just because this is a normal phase of life doesn't mean you shouldn't do anything about it. There's a lot riding on how you react. Some parents don't understand the changes their daughters are experiencing, so they criticise them and ride them hard. Unfortunately, that kind of reaction leaves scars that last a lifetime. The other extreme would be completely ignoring her, and that won't help, either.

Remember the puppy we were talking about? If your puppy chews up your new shoes, you don't automatically assume that it hates you or that you're a defective dog owner. You realise it's just doing what puppies do. It's a phase you have to get through. Try to look at your daughter the same way. She's having a hard time, and this is a phase you have to get through together.

Question: If I want to work on my anger, do I need to go back and analyse every instance when I lost my temper with someone or felt aggressive?

That kind of detailed memory work definitely helps as long as you can do it objectively. Try to think of the person who made you angry as Object A and yourself as Object B. Then analyse the movement of those two objects and how they affected each other. If you can't do that—if you keep thinking 'So-and-so is such a bitch. I can't believe she treated me like that'—then you'll never be able to analyse the situation and understand the causes. If you want to unravel your anger, you first have to learn to keep your distance from the instances you analyse in your memory. You have to act like an observer.

If you can't do that, try imagining someone else in your place. So, instead of you and your friend, imagine your friend and a third person. Walk through what happened step by step and see how the two people affected each other. You can even draw a diagram of the situation on paper. But don't let yourself get upset. Keep that bird's eye view. Don't assume that your friend was out of line for whatever they said or did. Remind yourself that millions of people just like them would have behaved the same. Now, try imagining that you behaved differently. How would they have reacted? Ask yourself what your friend needs from you and what you need from them.

Once you give yourself some distance from the situation, you'll understand what happened and what you should do next. When I wrote my first books, that's exactly how I found the solutions to the problems people came to me with. I diagrammed them on paper and analysed them until they made sense. That's all you have to do.

Question: Why is it so hard to show people how out of line they are in the moment when they're angry?

Because anger short-circuits a person's awareness. When a person is angry, they're under the effect of a powerful instinct. That's the whole point. Calling them to reason using words won't work, because they just can't hear you. Wait for them to calm down, and then you can show them the damage they're doing. But you have to wait for them to cool off. As long as they're angry, they're unstable and unaware of what other people around them are feeling.

Question: Can you tell us more about what you feel when you pick up on a person's anger?

That brings me back to my favourite topic: frequencies. On a regular day, I'm on a positive frequency and I see everything that happens around me with calm detachment. Like I'm a passenger in a car watching different landscapes go past my window. I see two people kissing on a street corner. I see an old lady trying to cross the street. I see a teenager flying down the sidewalk on a skateboard. I see a tired face looking out the window of a bus. And I look on all these people with kindness.

But if the person in the car with me is negative, I start to feel afraid or even annoyed. This affects everything I see when I look out the window. I sense the danger on my skin.

We've already talked about what can cause anger, but I'd like to look at it from the other side: what if you're the one people are getting angry at? Maybe you don't have any anger inside of you, but you frequently cause others to be angry at you. That's a problem. It's true that some of the time that anger has nothing to do with you, but you should also ask yourself if this is nature's way of hinting that you need to work on yourself. Are you pushy or demanding or forgetful? The boiling, hurtful anger that people have inside is their problem—that's a fact. But that doesn't mean you can provoke them without getting hurt. This is an important thing to think about, and we'll come back to it again later.

Question: What do you mean when you say that a person who has all these negative traits is rotting inside? I'm asking because I've noticed that my acne gets worse when I let my anger be in control.

Most people accept the idea that if you worry too much or let yourself get too angry, it can affect your health. What happens when you're upset? You're out of balance. Out of harmony. Anger is a heavy burden to carry. Over time, it weakens you physically. You start to fall apart, like a car that no one takes care of. Maybe your eyesight suddenly gets worse, or your skin breaks out, or your back starts giving you trouble. Psychosomatic conditions are a real thing. The people who keep calm and have cool heads are the ones who live long, healthy lives. It doesn't matter if they smoke and eat meat three times a day, they'll still live into their eighties. But if you're always irritated by something, your body will suffer the damage.

Here's a more practical thing to consider: when you're angry all the time, you drop your cell phone, bang your knee against a table, crash your car, fall down the stairs…it's all related because of your unbalanced, unstable mind.

Lust

Sex is a hard thing for a lot of people to talk about, and that discomfort extends to lust, too. It's an uncomfortable topic, isn't it? When I was younger, I never could get any of the adults around me to explain what the word 'lust' meant, but it sounded bad, so I assumed it was something indecent or rude. The same thing happens in families around the world: parents don't want to talk about sex, much less lust, so kids never really understand how they differ.

If you look back at Greek mythology or any other pantheon of deities in history, they all had multiple husbands or wives and scores of children. That's one thing I want you to consider.

The second thing I want you to consider is the fact that the human race still exists. We may be afraid of talking about sex, but we aren't afraid of doing it.

Here's the revelation: sex and lust are not the same thing. No deity ever forbade humans from having sex. After all, without sex we wouldn't exist. The sinful element in lust is the *untruth* at the heart of it. Hear me out. Let's say you chose a person to spend your life with and had a family with them. After a while, though, you found someone else attractive—you experienced lust—and committed adultery. Adultery is a lie. And lies always come out in the end, because nature doesn't believe in lying. Lies take up your attention. They block your mind and keep you from growing. So those lies always get found out, 100% of the time. As a result, there's no logic in lying. You always lose.

But here's the paradox, and this is going to sound wild to some of you: if you're living with a partner and are open about your interest in another person, even if you spend time with that other person, even if you sleep with that other person, you haven't done anything wrong. Why? Because you didn't lie about it. You are risking your original relationship by telling the truth, because 99% of the time your partner is not going to stay with you since you have this interest in someone else. But as long as you haven't lied, you haven't done anything bad.

If you choose to lie about your interest in another person, then your sexual interest in them—which could have been neutral—becomes lust. I'm not recommending that you go find a new sex partner and tell your spouse or partner about it. I just want to illustrate the difference between sex and lust so that it makes sense to you.

Just like anger is all about your feelings, lust is all about your intentions. Most people today are serial monogamists. We stay with a single partner until we move on to someone else. There's nothing wrong with that. There's nothing wrong with having sex just for the sex, as long as there's mutual understanding about your intentions. Where lust comes into play is when you pursue sex with a person with the intention of using or hurting them. Lust would be having sex with a partner who wants to get married and have a family while hiding the fact that you don't want any of those things. Another example of lust would be pursuing a person who is naive and inexperienced because you just want to have sex with them. In both cases, you're using that person for sex without their consent.

But it's a fine line. If you're committed to personal growth, then you shouldn't be wasting your energy on a million different sex partners, even if they are all as enthusiastic as you are. Constantly needing attention from the opposite sex puts you on a lower frequency. That makes it hard for you to build a solid relationship with someone. After all, the people you socialise with are just looking for casual sex.

You'd be better off staying single and cultivating sincere friendships with other people who want to grow and improve themselves. If that leads to a relationship and sex, then so be it. That's a bonus. It wasn't your intention. Just don't look at dating and sex as a sport where you score points. That's lust. It's an addiction, and it makes you weak.

The Bible tells us that sex before marriage is a sin. I take that with a grain of salt. Remember, the Bible is just one source, and it may not have the whole story. It certainly doesn't cover all the different ways that people have viewed sex across cultures and millennia. We know from ancient texts that the gods and demigods were all having plenty of sex. I don't see any reason for modern people to abstain from sex for the first thirty years of their lives or get married at sixteen just so they can have some fun. That's ridiculous. There's nothing spiritually pure about waiting to have sex until you've graduated from college, found a job, and bought a house. I think we're pretty safe saying that the Bible was misinterpreted.

The Christian philosopher Thomas Aquinas wrote that all the forms of lust go against nature and reason. Dictionary definitions of lust highlight the fact that lust is overwhelming and can't be controlled. I want to look closely at what that means in real life. If you have an animalistic desire for a person, that's a sin. But if your desire is conscious and aware, if your heart is involved in the process, then it isn't a sin. It isn't lust. When a person touches another person with love, the feelings are deep and sincere. Their heart is doing the work. But a person just desires another person's body for sex, then that person is a demon with a depraved mind.

There are two kinds of people: the ones who have sex, and the ones who make love. When you meet someone and they just want to hop into bed with you without showing any affection or talking or getting to know you, that's a sign that they are in lust, not in love.

Aquinas took a practical approach to lust. He looked at the things lust makes people do and divided them into categories: fornication, adultery, incest, seduction, and rape. Fornication is defined as sex between unmarried partners, but how can we look at that today? Here's my take: fornication has nothing to do with whether or not you got a marriage license before sleeping with someone. That would be a superficial way of understanding it. To understand what Aquinas meant, you have to think about responsibility. If you care about the person you're having sex with and are interested in them for who they are, then you're being responsible. You aren't guilty of fornication. But if your sole interest in your partner is physical, then that's fornication because you're being irresponsible.

The second item in the list is adultery—having sex with a person who already has a partner. Here's an important thing to realise: Aquinas didn't list adultery as a type of sinful lust because of the damage it does to the person or persons who are cheated on. He listed it as a sin because of the effect it has on the two people committing adultery together. If you push someone to commit adultery with you, you're encouraging them to sin.

Incest is the next item. We all understand that it's wrong to be sexually interested in a family member. Incest happens when a person doesn't care who they have sex with. They'll even use a member of their own family to satisfy their lust. It's a terrible thing.

Seduction is the next kind of lust, and Aquinas defined it as having sex with a virgin. That doesn't seem like a hard thing to avoid in today's world. But I caution you against viewing this legalistically. You can't just be a life hacker and only have sex with non-virgins with the idea that you aren't sinning. If your heart isn't involved, the sex is still a symptom of sinful lust.

The fifth kind of lust Aquinas described is rape, or non-consensual sex. I hope that everyone who is here with me for this discussion of sins and virtues understands that rape is wrong. That much ought to be clear by now.

Let's turn back to the Bible for a moment. In Matthew, chapter 5, verses 27-32, we find this: "You have heard it said, 'You shall not commit adultery.' But I tell you that anyone who looks at a woman lustfully has already committed adultery with her in his heart. If your right eye causes you to stumble, gouge it out and throw it away. It is better for you to lose one part of your body than for your whole body to be thrown into hell. And if your right hand causes you to stumble, cut it off and throw it away. It is better for you to lose one part of your body than for your whole body to go to hell. It has been said, 'Anyone who divorces his wife must give her a certificate of divorce.' But I tell you that anyone who divorces his wife, except for sexual immorality, makes her the victim of adultery, and anyone who marries a divorced woman commits adultery."

There is a lot to think about in those verses about how we are supposed to relate to potential sex partners. I've already talked about how I had a hard time in school and college because all the other men were talking dirty about women. I always felt like I was doing something wrong just by sitting next to a guy who was being vulgar about women. To some extent, that experience drove me to study how society works and write books. But at first, it was difficult for me emotionally. A man who allows himself to be vulgar about women—and by vulgar I mean treating women like objects you insert your penis into—isn't being led by his soul. His fire has already gone out, and he vibrates on the frequencies dictated by society or by his mind. That's where the preoccupation with sex comes from. When you look at people of the opposite sex and your first reaction is sexual, that's a bad thing.

When I was working with frequencies, I noticed a curious correlation: if I connected to the mind's frequency or society's frequency, I could get a better read on those people. And I also found that being on those frequencies caused me to think more about sex and to desire the women around me. It was a troubling experience. But when I connected to the frequency I created—which I call 'Peace'—I found that all those external thoughts and desires went away and I was able to relate to women with my true heart. When you're on the Peace frequency, you don't have those vulgar, objectifying thoughts and desires.

The more you learn about frequencies, the more you realise that you can live the life of the mind or you can live the life beyond the mind. When you turn on your heart and live on a pure frequency, you don't objectify the people around you, and you aren't preoccupied with sex. If you live by society's rules, you will always be fighting those things.

So, if you notice you have these immediate, unfounded sexual reactions to the people around you, understand that you are being led by your mind. Your mind is amplifying this particular negative quality. A little later in this book, I'll give you a list of ways to deal with the sexual obsession, but for now, I want us to focus on the cause and effect. Where it all comes from.

Questions and Answers about Lust

Question: What about creative people who radiate sensuality? The kind of people who fall in love easily and other people fall in love with them, too. What can a person like that do to avoid tempting others? And how can we avoid being tempted by them?

You're confusing love and lust, which are two very different concepts. Let's say the person you're asking about is a woman. Ask yourself: is she attracting people's attention because she dresses erotically? Is she tempting people on purpose? Is she posting suggestive photos on social media? If so, that's closer to lust. That's sexual manipulation. On the other hand, if she's attracting attention because she's kind and charismatic and radiates warmth, there's nothing wrong with that. She isn't guilty of tempting anyone, and the people who fall in love with her aren't guilty of lust. They're just naturally attracted to the good that is in her.

People who follow their own hearts will not be tempted by anything vulgar. When someone posts nude photos on social media, people with pure hearts are turned off by that. It has nothing to do with willpower, because we all are weak to some extent. It's about living in darkness and being attracted to darkness. And once you indulge one negative characteristic, it becomes easier for other negative characteristics to take root in your life. That's how it works.

Again, the question confuses love, which comes from the heart, with lust, which comes from the mind. Imagine that I fall in love with someone and we're together for six months. During that time, we have sex and we're happy. But eventually we part ways. I'm on my own for a couple of months, and then I fall in love again and it lasts for a year this time. Is that lust? Not as long as I'm being sincere and following my heart. My heart leads me. With lust, my mind is in control and I just want the sex and not the whole person. Try not to confuse those concepts.

Question: Is it sinful to have sex for money or to act in porn films?

Most definitely. Prostitution and pornography both belong to the world of temptation and vice. They exist on a low frequency. People come to prostitution by different roads. Some of them end up there because of negative behaviours they were engaging in, but others get pulled in because they were in desperate straits and someone told them that prostitution was the way out.

It's a bad frequency that often involves drug use. And it's definitely fuelled by lust. Good people with warm hearts don't search out prostitutes. You have to be dark inside to buy sex. Again, that darkness isn't necessarily a lifelong affliction. Maybe their loved one passed away, or they lost their job, or they got a terminal diagnosis, and they're kind of adrift. When things like that happen to a person, they are at risk of being pulled in the wrong direction. Imagine a man whose wife died, and one day he runs into a childhood friend who lives on the dark side, and this friend says, "Let's go get a beer." The friend's next suggestion might be to text a prostitute to meet them at his place. The guy goes along with it because he feels lost and aimless, and anything seems better than the emptiness in his life.

But that's a dangerous choice, because as we've already discussed, one negative action brings with it more negative actions. When we choose negative energy, we surround ourselves with negative people who feed us with more of the things that are bad for us.

Most of the questions people send me about lust are specifically about prostitution, pornography, and masturbation. I want you to understand that talking about these subjects—even thinking about them—is bad for you. The more I tell you about masturbation, the more you're going to think about it. So, I'll just say a few words about pornography in response to this question, and then I will move on to the next question.

If you live on the frequency of the heart, you'll find pornography disgusting. If you're interested in happiness, love, and children, you won't be interested in pornography. It's that simple.

What about porn actors? Here's my answer: if you're already in the business, then you should try to get out; if you aren't in the business yet, don't get sucked in. Working in porn will automatically tune you to a frequency where you get involved in drugs and other criminal behaviour. It's a terrible world to be in.

Before you say that prostitution—and, by association, pornography—is one of the oldest professions, hear me out. All the sins we are considering have been around forever. And that's normal, but that doesn't make it right. This world is a school, and we are here to learn. None of us are perfect. Our job is to understand our own negative characteristics and learn how to get rid of them. So, stay away from prostitution, pornography, all of it. Don't be a consumer and don't be a producer of either.

I can hear you wondering if it's ok to just watch porn sometimes. Sure, go ahead. No one is stopping you. But every time you watch pornography, you get pulled down to a lower frequency. And the more unresolved negative issues you already have in your life, the more dangerous that is. If I'm 99% pure, watching a single porn film won't have an irreversible effect on me. But most people aren't anywhere near 99% pure, are they? That's what makes pornography dangerous: when you're already weak, it pulls you further down.

I've noticed that when people stay within the framework of their normal lives, they're much less likely to be tempted by lust, whether in the form of masturbation or irresponsible sex or an interest in pornography or prostitution.

What do I mean by framework? I mean that when a person listens to their usual music and hangs out with their normal friend group, they don't have that preoccupation with lust. But as soon as they start hanging out with different people, eating different food, and listening to different music, their lustful desires become much stronger. Pay attention and you may notice this happens to you.

Question: If a person has a pure heart, does that mean that lustful people won't be attracted to them or try to tempt them?

Temptations surround us every day. That's a fact. But a less-evolved person will face infinitely more temptations on a daily basis than a person who has cleaned out their heart. I always put it this way: the cleaner you are, the less crap you attract. It's true. Once you climb out of the world of liars, cheaters, and egoists, you'll have fewer people in your life who are trying to trip you up. But that doesn't mean that you'll never face temptation, or that you'll never face devils. You have to always be prepared.

The devil will always provoke you right when you're getting close to enlightenment, because he wants to tempt you and drive you off the path to goodness. We are always at a crossroads. We are always making choices. You can't expect to sit back and take it easy once you achieve a higher frequency. The difference is that you won't also be dealing with negative people and situations that you brought on yourself. It does get easier.

When I studied the question of hell, I was living in hell alongside shallow, soulless egotists. If you live in society on the lowest frequency, people are always trying to betray you and hurt you. Once you move up to a higher frequency in society, the damage is still there but it's less. When I first started studying frequencies, I decided to travel around and try them all. My mentor warned me to be careful, because there are frequencies where truly awful things happen.

I'm not talking about just meeting new people. I'm talking about travelling to different frequencies where there are people you wouldn't normally meet. Eventually, I discovered that I could live on any number of those frequencies. I observed how my life changed on each frequency. It wasn't just my mood and my feelings. Even my physical sensations and my health changed. But I remembered my mentor's warning about staying away from the evil people you meet on the lowest frequencies, so after a while I limited myself to the higher frequencies.

Question: What if I like having sex because it's pleasurable?

Pleasures are bad for you. All of them. If I walk into a nice restaurant and talk to people my age, almost every single one of them will say that they build their life around their pleasures. They eat because they enjoy food. They worship it. That's bad. They base their relationships on pleasure and on their own needs. It's all 'me-me-me.' Pleasure is a terrible foundation for a life.

If your goal is to earn passive income and sit on the beach all day, you're in for a rude awakening: that's a sinful way to live, because all you're doing is consuming. Taking. You aren't doing anything for the rest of us. When you're a consumer, you only consider your own pleasure. What about the community around you? What about the angels and the gods? You won't have time to think about them. What's the point of being born if all you do is consume? We know that living like a consumer is wrong because it goes against the very logic of the system. We are supposed to be striving and growing. That's the whole point.

If you strive to cleanse your heart and mind, you'll find that your interest in sex changes. Right now, you're interested in chasing pleasure. And you're not alone. Most people are sick at heart and feel afraid. They worry that they have to compete with everyone all the time. So, they turn to sex for pleasure and consolation. But once you achieve some enlightenment you don't need sex as constant reinforcement.

Question: What happens when a lustful person seduces someone who didn't already have lust in their heart?

The lustful person ruins the person they seduce. That's exactly what we used to call it: ruining someone. When the other person allows themselves to be seduced, then a code inside them turns on and they'll never be the same.

Question: Whose fault is it if someone commits adultery because...

I have to interrupt here. Adultery—or any other romantic betrayal—is always fuelled by lust. We don't have time to pick apart all the psychological factors in adultery. There are a million possible causes, and you can always flip the situation to make either partner look guilty. If your significant other is cheating on you, they are the one in the wrong. Or are you maybe in the wrong because you froze them out or didn't give them enough attention? See how that works? It can go either way. But I don't think any of that matters. You have to accept the facts of what happened. Trying to establish guilt is a function of resentment. In the end, it doesn't matter whose fault it was.

You have to decide what kind of life you want to have. Do you want to be constantly criticising your partner? Because that's easy enough to accomplish. Lots of people do it. Or would you rather live in harmony and equality with your partner? You can do that, too. But first you have to become that kind of person, and then you have to find that kind of partner.

The message is simple: if your partner is a jerk who cheats on you, that's your world. You built it yourself, and if you don't like it you can leave and build a different world with a different person. In order for that to work, though, you have to purify your heart and try to live on a higher frequency.

There are 144 types of relationships, and they all have their nuances. Why is that? Because there are 12 frequencies and 12 sub-frequencies. Just imagine all the combinations. Especially since we all start from very different places when we enter relationships. Some people are acting on instinct, while others are motivated by lust or love. Some jump into relationships because they're afraid of being alone, while others look for someone they can fight with because that's the only way they know how to live. So, there is an infinite variety of relationships.

Remember that adultery is always fuelled by lust. If you live with a person and lie to them about spending time with someone else, that's lust. That's sin.

To be honest, lust is my least favourite sin to write about. It's the one that people tend to have an unhealthy interest in. More people write in with questions about lust than any other issue. It gets people's juices flowing. But writing about it makes me upset, and reading about it is likely to pull you down to a lower frequency.

Question: Is it lust if a committed couple plays sex games together?

Not at all. Back in the 1950s, sex was supposed to happen in the dark under a heavy blanket, but that was a cultural fixation, not a moral rule. If you're having consensual sex with a partner you love, with the person who is your other half, then there's nothing wrong with playing games or using toys or doing anything else that you both feel good about. Remember, lust doesn't have anything to do with a particular sex act. It's just an unhealthy preoccupation with sex when you aren't interested in the other person or thinking about what is best for them.

Question: Can lust be a motivating force in a person's life like envy and pride?

Sure, it can, but only in a very shallow way. People who suffer from the sin of lust are obsessed with bodies—their own and everybody else's. So, they work out and watch their weight to look their best. I guess you could say that's a benefit, but only on the surface. When a lustful person has sex with a good-looking partner, it's like they're copulating with a beautiful image. All they see are the externalities.

A person who lives by the heart has a different system of values. They see past skin and hair and abs to what people really have inside them. They want to get to know people in a meaningful way.

So, while lust can motivate someone to make positive changes in their life, all those changes will be on the surface. Nothing deep.

Question: What does it mean if I'm in a relationship but I'm attracted to other men? I don't want to have sex with them. I just want to be around and talk with other men I find interesting.

That's a good question, and I can tell you want to do the right thing. Here's the good news: wanting to socialise with men other than your partner has nothing to do with lust. You could be married with kids and still enjoy platonic friendships with men outside your marriage. The same is true of your boyfriend. There's nothing wrong with him socialising with other women.

Jealousy is a strong instinct for many people, but you have to look at it logically. Right now, I'm single and I have plenty of friends of both genders. Am I supposed to stop talking to my female friends the instant I change my relationship status? That would be ridiculous. Or what if I see a good TED talk and reach out to the speaker to talk about collaborating, but she is—gasp—a woman? Do you see how silly that thinking is? You're trying to do the right thing, but you're misunderstanding where the problem actually lies.

If you're truthful and sincere, if you have no hidden intentions or deceitful plans, then there's nothing wrong with having friends of the opposite sex.

Friendships outside your relationship are wonderful if you treat people as individuals worthy of respect. It's that simple.

Your question boils down to this: can a man and a woman be friends? My answer is a resounding yes.

Question: If I'm separated from my spouse but not officially divorced yet, would it be adultery for me to start a new relationship?

You have a paperwork issue, not a morality issue. The root of adultery is dishonesty, and the date on a piece of paper has nothing to do with it. If I understand your question correctly, you and your former spouse have gone your separate ways and are each building a new life. Even if you don't have the official paperwork yet, both of you know the old relationship is over and you can start a new relationship with a clear conscience.

Question: How can I tell if the person I'm dating has another relationship that they're hiding from me?

If this question has anything to do with lust, then it's on your end, not your partner's. Why? Because the only way to discover if your partner has another relationship they aren't telling you about is to get to know them. Spend time with them. Look for signs of honesty. Do they disappear for days at a time without a good explanation? That's a strong warning sign. Do they introduce you to their family and friends? Can you contact them any time, day or night? Those are all good signs.

Don't have sex with a person until you're sure they are decent and kind. It's that simple.

And if you do find out that your partner has another relationship on the side, that relationship is not your responsibility. Any pain they cause in that relationship is their fault.

Question: What if one partner in a relationship wants more sex than the other?

People are different. If you and your partner are both pure, creative people, you can build a life together based on your interests and your work. But if you're a pure person and you live with someone who suffers from lust, then they're going to be unhappy. They're going to start by demanding more sex, and eventually they'll leave you for someone else. That's just how it works.

Question: Do we get punished for causing another person to lust?

If you and your partner both suffer from lust, then you're at the same level together. Neither of you is dragging the other one down, so nobody's going to get punished. If, on the other hand, you're a lustful person and you seduce someone who is pure and clean, then you're acting like a devil and you'll be punished. How does that work? Every time you sin, you collect negative points that start to add up. Collect enough negative points and something bad happens. The opposite is also true: every time you do something good, you earn positive points. Earn enough positive points and something delightful will come your way. It's simple, really.

Question: If lust has been a problem for me in the past, is there a way I can get clean?

Of course. Lust is really dependent on the people you have around you. If you change the crowd you hang out with and look for good people with pure hearts, you'll find that your lust withers away. You'll also find that you're better able to concentrate and meditate. Lust is powered by your mind, so if you take yourself out of that atmosphere that is conducive to lust, you'll notice you can pay attention better. Maybe even meditate for the first time. I've worked with people who had a hard time turning off their brains to meditate, and that's always a sign that you have some unresolved sins. It's a vicious cycle: your mind fuels the sin, and the sin keeps your mind busy so you can't focus on anything. The good news is that once you deal with the underlying sin, you'll be able to meditate. That's how it works.

Here's another thing to think about: most people who write in with questions are worried about their relationships. Everybody's in a hurry to find somebody to be with, and then they realise they're unhappy with that person. They put up with each other for a while, then they start arguing, and eventually they break up. If it's really bad, they all end up getting prescriptions for something to make them feel better. Don't be in such a hurry to find a significant other. Take it slow.

Work on yourself first. Then look around until you find a person you're sure about. Ask yourself if you're prepared to be responsible for that person. Are they prepared to be responsible for you? Do they really know you? Let them see all of you, not just the shiny, awesome parts. Tell them all about your shortcomings. If they stick around, then there's a chance the two of you might work well together.

    Find out why they want to be in a relationship with you. This is incredibly important. Don't bother trying to build a relationship with someone who's just in it because they're bored and don't have anything else to do, or because they're afraid to be alone. I find it interesting how many of my readers write in about relationship problems. Here I am with years of experience studying life and its problems and I still don't feel ready to settle down with another person. It's a big step, but so many people just rush headlong into it. So, don't do that. Don't pair up with someone because you're bored and need someone to entertain you. I promise you'll be sorry if you do.

Gluttony

Gluttony is a psychological dependence on food. Overeating is a tool people use to deaden their senses, because food is numbing. It may feed your mind and body, but it numbs your soul. People who eat too much are addicted to pleasure, which is bad, or they don't want to feel whatever they have in their souls. All those people who are constantly posting photos of the food they eat and the pools they sit by—we don't need those people. They aren't contributing anything to life on earth. If aliens took them tomorrow, the rest of us wouldn't be any worse off.

Food is a necessity and nothing more. Don't overeat, and don't be picky about what you eat, either. You want to get to a place where you can listen to your body and eat a healthy meal when you're hungry without making a big deal about it. No photos of your plate. And no guilt afterwards, either. Just eat the food and move on to the next thing.

I expect someone's going to ask me if the chef at a five-star restaurant is a terrible person because they think about food all the time. Of course not. Cooking can be an art form. But that's not what we're talking about. Gluttony is not about wanting your food to be delicious and look beautiful. It's about using food to fill up the empty places in your heart.

Questions and Answer about Gluttony

Question: Is it gluttony if I love looking at food that's beautifully plated?

No, gluttony is specifically overeating. Eating beyond what you need to survive. If you get pleasure from seeing a beautiful plate of sashimi or a green salad with toasted nuts and deep red radicchio, that's aesthetic enjoyment, not gluttony. There might be a little pride involved if you go to a lot of trouble to plate your food just so you can impress other people. But if you're doing it for your own enjoyment, there's nothing at all wrong with that.

Being picky about food is another form of gluttony. When you're picky, you want something from the food beyond its ability to keep you alive. You want it to be made of certain ingredients or leave out things you don't like. That attitude toward food is the opposite of what it should be, and it's sinful. Why? Because any time you make an idol out of food—either because you eat so much of it or because you're so fussy about it—you're turning away from God.

Question: Sometimes, I get intense cravings for specific things. Is that gluttony?

Cravings are gluttony if you act on them, because they're unnatural and take your attention away from more important things. Here's an extreme example to help you make sense of this: bowel movements are natural. Everybody has them. But it would be unnatural if you only wanted to have your morning bowel movement while seated in the lotus position in your backyard. Do you see the difference? Gluttony works the same way. If you need to eat something, then eat something. But don't make a big deal about it. Don't run out to the store to satisfy a craving. Don't be overbearing about picking the restaurant you go to with your friends. Just let food happen. Tell your friends you'll go wherever they want. If you're at home, open the fridge and eat something that you know will nourish your body.

Question: What if I have to follow a special diet for health reasons?

I'm not a doctor, so all my advice is targeted at reasonably healthy people. If you're sick, I don't want you to jump out of bed and go hang out with your friends just because you read in one of my books that socialising is good for you. If you have to follow a special diet, then do that. I just want everyone to understand that the act of eating should never be something you obsess about. Buy healthy food you can afford, prepare it simply, and eat enough of it to meet your needs. Anything above that is gluttony.

Question: Is it gluttony when a person doesn't observe religious fasts, such as for Lent?

No, it isn't. If you observe the fasts because it makes sense for you spiritually, then that's wonderful. But you shouldn't force yourself to fast. Forcing yourself never works.

This is where I believe my books are valuable. Anyone can tell you what the rules are. There are library shelves full of books that tell you what to do and what not to do. My information is different, because I explain where your sinful desires come from, what makes them stronger, and how you can make them weaker and eventually get rid of them. I tell you exactly what elements to remove from your life in order to weaken the sins naturally. If your friend wants to lose weight and you tell them 'Just stop eating so much,' that isn't going to help. It might even make them eat more. Remember, you can't force yourself or anyone else to change. You have to investigate your life and find the things that feed your sinful desires. Once you get rid of those things, change happens naturally.

So, fasting is a wonderful practice if you come to it voluntarily. It's a great way to clear your head. But never force yourself or anyone else to fast.

Question: Maybe once a week I have a craving for a sweet or salty snack. Is that gluttony?

It is. Any time you're drawn to a specific food, that's gluttony. Especially if the food is something sweet. Sweets are addictive. Those thoughts suck up your energy and strengthen your mind at the expense of your heart. It's uncomfortable for people to feel what's in their souls, so they eat to deaden those feelings. Even positive, happy emotions.

Have you ever noticed how some people gain weight when they're stressed, while others lose weight? There may be a scientific explanation for this, but I think it can be explained fairly simply by my basic theory of how the mind reacts to stress. Stress causes some people's minds to go into overdrive. Their minds burn so many calories that they lose weight. Other people's minds shut down when they're stressed, and that sensation of absence, of the mind being gone, is so unfamiliar and unpleasant that they eat to try to restart their minds. And, of course, they gain weight. I'm not in the business of teaching people to lose weight, but if that's your personal goal, I want you to know that weight loss starts in the mind.

Question: I play sports and have to eat a lot to maintain muscle. That's not gluttony, is it?

Of course not. For your eating to be sinful, it has to be something you can't control. An animal reaction. That's how you can always tell the difference: ask yourself, is this something I need to do, or something I'm driven to do by an instinct I can't control? If you can go for a month without eating sweets, then you don't have a problem with gluttony. If you can't go for a month without sweets, or if you find yourself thinking about treats all the time, then you need to work on your gluttony. The same rule holds for any of the sins. If you can go for a month without having sex or watching porn, then you don't need to worry about lust. But if your thoughts turn to sex a thousand times a day, you have a problem.

Every civilisation in history has had warriors and athletes who paid attention to what they ate and drank to stay in top physical form. But here's the key point: athletes think about food to keep their bodies in shape. Not because you can't stay away from the buffet.

Question: My friends and I enjoy cooking big dinners together and learning more about foods from around the world. That isn't gluttony, is it?

That's an excellent question, and the answer isn't straightforward. This whole book is about the path to spiritual growth, so any sin is something you need to work to free yourself from. Since you're here, that tells me you're already at a serious spiritual level. You're too advanced to still be worrying about expanding your awareness of what people in other countries are eating. Those interests and hobbies are worldly. Society is built on sin and encourages people to fixate on overeating, having sex, and earning money. But you're past that level. You can see that it's wrong.

At the same time, I don't want you to go overboard. I'm not a greedy person, but I have money in the bank. I don't suffer from gluttony, but I eat three times a day. And not the same thing at every meal, either. I like a little variety on my plate. But I don't make a fetish out of food. There's almost something childish about a preoccupation with food. Don't let yourself be controlled by your instincts. Treat food as something simple, something you do to stay healthy. It's only a sin when it becomes compulsive and tempting.

Cities are designed to get you to spend your money and time on worldly things. You can go from one bar or cafe to the next, all the way down the street. The economy is fuelled by sin. If you want to live on a higher, more spiritual frequency, though, you have to stop caring about worldly things like exotic foods and rare wines.

I went that route, myself. When I was a young teenager, everyone knew me when I walked down the street. I couldn't walk into a club without someone recognising me. But when I turned 18, I turned away from worldly things and started making videos and writing books. The people I used to hang out with all blocked me. No surprise there. And you know what? It didn't bother me at all. Because I surrounded myself with happy, pure people who valued me for my heart, not for the brand of shoes I wore. I made that choice.

Everyone told me I'd be poor for the rest of my life. That was fine with me. I just wanted to take pictures, listen to music, and write books. And I did well. Some of my former friends are still in shock about that. My belief was that I shouldn't waste myself. It's like lust: if you waste your energy on having sex with random people, you'll never meet that one special person. I didn't want to waste my energy on random work. So, I just sat down and did the work I knew I could do well. Undervaluing yourself and wasting your energy on things that don't matter is a sin.

Question: When something or someone annoys me, eating helps me feel calmer. Is that gluttony?

Any time something challenges you in life, you have a choice: you can suppress the uncomfortable feelings, or you can grow and overcome them. If you choose the first path, then just have a chocolate and you'll feel better. But if you choose the second path, you'll have to dig down and uncover exactly what bothers you about the situation. Then you can work on yourself until you're so strong that nothing about that situation makes you uncomfortable anymore.

What you described—using food for comfort—is a sin. Food shouldn't be a factor in your emotional life. If you are more likely to get upset when you haven't eaten, and eating makes you feel better, then you're experiencing one of the truest forms of gluttony.

Question: What are the negative effects of gluttony?

Gluttony, as I've explained, is harmful because it deadens your soul and strengthens your mind and all your animal instincts. That's the root of the problem. Gluttony closes you off from God, from faith, from your sense of your own inner self. When you let yourself be ruled by gluttony, you make decisions based on the workings of your mind instead of listening to your heart. You'll always be taking the wrong path, the wrong job, the wrong airplane. Everything will go wrong. Now, do you understand why it's called a deadly sin?

Question: I'm always reading articles about how we should eat this or that fruit or vegetable for the health benefits. Fish oil for inflammation. Nuts for brain health. Are you telling me not to pay attention to those recommendations?

The nutrition discourse is nothing but gluttony. Does that surprise you? Let me clarify: if your doctor gives you specific advice on what to eat and what not to eat to optimise your health, then you should follow that advice. If your coach or trainer wants you to eat a certain way to optimise your performance, then you should do that. But if you don't have those health or athletic reasons and you're always worrying about what you should eat, then that's just plain old picky eating. More and more people have these food fixations, and it's only gluttony in another form.

Question: Is snacking a kind of gluttony?

If you're snacking without thinking about it, without an objective reason for it, then yes, it's gluttony. I can see how snacking could be fine when you're travelling or working overtime and there isn't time for a meal, but otherwise you should eat mindfully when you need food instead of reaching for a snack because you're bored or stressed.

I'm going to digress here to talk about a phenomenon I associate with gluttony, although most people probably wouldn't think to call it that. What I have in mind is the trend toward psychiatry. Psychiatrists are prescribing antidepressants and other drugs to teenagers, even children. What does that have to do with gluttony? It's simple: when you go through a painful period in your life—maybe you're depressed or you have trouble focusing in school—you're supposed to suffer through it so you can grow. Your mind needs that suffering. It's necessary for your development. Especially when you're young. If you run to the doctor and get a prescription for something that improves your mood or helps you do better in school, you stunt your growth as a person. It's like picking a flower that hasn't opened yet and forcing the petals open with your fingers so you can see what's inside. Sure, you get to see inside the flower, but it isn't the same as what the experience could have been.

So, be careful before you trust the judgment of a stranger—who also is a mere mortal—who says you need to take medications to fix your mind. Anything that deadens your feelings is harmful and a form of gluttony.

Greed

Let's move on to talk about greed. Think of greed as this ravenous hunger for money or material things instead of food. A greedy person is someone who always wants more material wealth, even if they already have plenty. They'll walk all over anyone to get what they think they deserve. In this regard, greed is close to pride: they're both sins that involve seeing yourself as better than everyone else.

A person driven by greed can be immoral in other ways, too. They will hurt people to get their hands on money. They'll even break the law. But that doesn't mean that they're necessarily successful. Even an unsuccessful person can be greedy. It's your friend who always has to sit in the best chair in the room, the one who grabs the biggest piece of pizza (see how close that is to gluttony?). If someone offers you something for free, your greedy friend will jump in and claim it.

I'm lucky to work with a team of people who are the opposite of greedy. They're the people who would rather give than receive. But there are plenty of greedy people out there, and I'm sure you've encountered some of them.

Underneath the grasping and taking, greedy people suffer from a lack of self-confidence. If you're confident, you're happy and you don't need anything from anyone else. But if you're unsure of yourself, nothing you acquire will ever be enough. So, you become greedy, grasping at everything you see. One car isn't enough. You want five. Or six. Or seven, if you can manage it. That's greed.

Why is greed a sin? Because it's an instinct you can't control. You're empty inside, and you're trying to fill up that empty space with things. In essence, you're driven by fear. You're afraid that someone will take away what you have because you know you haven't lived honestly and well enough to deserve it.

Greed naturally occurs alongside envy and anger. When a greedy person sees that someone else is doing well or has things they wish they had, they immediately experience envy and anger.

That's the paradox: as soon as you fall prey to one sin, you're more likely to come down with the others, too. But when you work on a single negative trait, even starting with something that's easy for you, the other traits naturally become weaker. They're all tied together.

Questions and Answers about Greed

Question: I'm starting my own business, and my business plan states that my goal is to make as much money as fast as possible. Is that sinful? Are you saying I should just pick a business that helps others and wait to see if it makes me any money?

It sounds that way, doesn't it? But let me explain. I've been a consultant for over ten years, and I've seen that the very people who go into business for the money are the ones who are the least likely to succeed. When a client tells me, "I'm launching a start-up and I'm going to make a killing," I just shake my head. If they aren't launching that start-up because they're keen to deliver a product, if all they're thinking about is money, there's no way they will be successful. They're tripping themselves up before they even get started. Life punishes us when we behave like that. Every single time.

If your goals are materialistic—a beach house, an expensive sports car, passive income—then you're ruled by greed. You're empty inside and trying to show off.

Working to earn money isn't a sin. Here's an example: maybe you went to trade school and partnered with a buddy and started making custom outdoor kitchens and pool cabanas for people to put in their yards. Even after taxes and overhead, you can make good money in that kind of business without dancing on TikTok or anywhere else. It's honest work for honest pay. But a lot of people wouldn't even consider your nice little business a success. They want easy money that hits their bank accounts while they sleep. They used to flip houses. Now, they buy bitcoin. Anything they think will turn a profit with little actual effort. They sign up for passive income classes and read books on passive income. Every lazy fool out there wants to strike it rich without actually working.

If you want to go into business, be serious about it. Put your heart and soul into it. Sell something that people need, something you would be happy to buy for yourself. Make something you can be proud of. Do you see the difference? Working hard and making good money is wonderful. Trying to get your hands on money without working is just greed.

Question: Where is the line between virtuous business and sinful business? What if my business involves buying low and selling high?

Honesty—or the lack thereof—is what draws the line. Let's say you hire a company to build your new site, and they charge you $5,000. In reality, they're only paying their employees $2,500 for the time it takes to build your site, plus some overhead. So, they're making a tidy profit. That's the first scenario. The second scenario is this: you call your friend who builds websites and ask him to find someone to take on your project. The friend calls you back a couple of days later and tells you they negotiated hard for you and got you a deal: the site's going to cost you $5,000. In reality, your friend is paying someone $2,500 to do the work and is pocketing the difference. Any negotiating they did was solely for their own benefit. In the first example, there's nothing wrong with a company charging what it feels its services are worth. In the second example, your friend is being dishonest at your expense. It's the lack of honesty that makes the difference, not the size of the markup.

Here's another example. You're in the business of buying a commodity. Grain, for example. Your supplier tells you that the grain you want costs $100,000, but you'll have to pay an extra $50,000 for shipping because of supply chain issues that are making it hard to get the right container for the grain. If that's true, then there's nothing wrong or dishonest about the supplier's business practices. But, on the other hand, if they actually have the grain you need sitting in a warehouse and they're just up charging you because everyone's talking about the supply chain and they figure you won't question it, then that's sinful.

So, there's nothing inherently wrong with what you want to do. You can buy low and sell high, as long as you're honest about what you're doing. Charge what the market will bear, but don't lie to make it look like you're working harder or spending more than you are.

When I self-publish a book, I can charge $10 for it, or I can charge $1,000 for it. It's my product, so I get to decide the price. That's how I find out what the market will bear. When you buy lunch at the airport, you pay three times more for it than you would in a neighbourhood cafe. That isn't greed—the price just reflects the seller's higher rent and the fact that people are willing to pay more for food at the airport, where there aren't as many choices.

Let's say I travel the world collecting antiques and then turn around and sell the whole collection to an interior designer at a profit of 1,000%. That isn't greed. The price reflects my effort, my talent, and the money and time I spent putting together the collection. If the interior designer doesn't like my price, they can travel to Central Asia and pick out their own antiques.

It gets more complicated if you don't have set prices. I've dealt with sellers who raise their prices when they see you have money. That's greed. Who cares if the buyer is a member of parliament or a bus driver? In my own business, if a consultation costs $200, then that's the price for anyone who wants that consultation. It's more honest that way.

When we lie about money, we're acting on greed. If you buy a fleet of delivery vans for $10,000 each and tell a potential buyer that they're worth $20,000, that's greed. But if you just charge $20,000 because that's a fair price that people are willing to pay, then there's nothing greedy about that.

Have you ever been to a farmer's market or craft fair and bought a handmade mug? Most of the ceramic artists you see at those places live hand to mouth, or they have a day job that pays the bills. But let's say you make handmade coffee mugs and you put more time and skill into the work and more effort into your marketing. Pretty soon, you're doing hundreds of thousands of dollars a month in sales. How is that possible? It's because you're on a higher frequency than the other artists. Maybe your colours and proportions are spot-on, or you're good at presenting your work to buyers at the right stores. In any case, you're doing better than the others because you're smart and talented, not because you're greedy.

I hope these examples make it clear that greed is about wanting more than you're entitled to, not about simply making money.

Question: Is it greedy to make friends with people because of what they can do for you?

Of course, it is. Any time you do something not for its own sake, not for your own enjoyment or spiritual or mental betterment, then you're motivated by sin. If you make friends with someone, attend an event, or even just post a photograph with the intention of promoting or benefiting your own interests, then that's greed pure and simple.

Attending a certain college because you want to find a wealthy spouse is greed. Making friends with someone because they can help you access capital for your business is greed. It's all about your intentions. Ninety-nine out of a hundred people are motivated by sin this way. Some people have one type of sin that motivates them, while others have two or even three. This is especially true of anyone who achieves the kind of wealth and fame that makes society look up to them. Don't be fooled by what you see of their lives. And don't look at what they have through the lens of your own sin. Because when you think success means having a lot of money, then you have a sinful understanding of success.

You wouldn't be alone, though. Almost everyone thinks too much about money. The desire for money has nothing to do with your financial status. Rich people want money just as badly as poor people do. It's all about greed and sin.

If you cleanse yourself of the sin of greed, then you won't care if you make $20,000 a year or $20 million. That won't be the most important factor in your life anymore, because you'll be living by your heart. As long as you suffer from greed, nothing will be enough: not the $20,000 and not even the $20 million. You'll always need more. But if you free yourself from greed, then you won't notice how much money you have.

Here's an interesting thing to consider: once money is no longer the driving force in your life, you won't have a price on your head anymore. People won't assume that they can show you the money and you'll jump for it. Think about how that would change your life.

I hope you're starting to understand that anyone—not just rich and successful people—can be greedy. Anyone who is preoccupied with money, whether or not they have a lot of it, suffers from greed. Unfortunately, that describes most people. The more money they have, the more they worry about money. It's a never-ending cycle. They blame their families, their friends, their boss at work, and even the government for their own weakness. If you have a pure heart and trust in God, on the other hand, you'll always be well.

Question: Is greed like anger in the sense that if you give in to it once, it will take root in you and become worse over time?

That's an excellent question. Greed works the same way as anger. There's no 'getting away with it' one time. Every action you take affects your future, and when you act on greed, you essentially build in greed to your life from that point on. And once you let greed in, it will start to strengthen all your other negative characteristics. It's a snowball effect fuelled by lack of awareness.

The seven sins are animal instincts that control your mind. Once you free yourself from them, you'll be able to see with new eyes, and you'll experience the joy of heaven right here on earth. You will no longer be afraid or angry, and you'll gain creative powers beyond anything you ever dreamed of. You won't care about what you look like or how much money you have. You won't be ashamed of living in a tiny apartment, or even your parents' basement. You'll just ride the wave of creativity that comes with self-acceptance.

But all it takes is one sinful act for all of that to fall apart, and once again you'll be scared and angry and ignorant because you'll be able to see all the demons again. That's how it works.

So, you see, cleansing yourself of sin is the most direct route to the joy that every civilisation has been striving toward for all of human history, each by its own methods. This is what I've been talking about and writing about my entire adult life. On the one hand, getting rid of sin is easy. On the other hand, it's a long and difficult path. You have to know how your mind works and how the world works. You have to know what all the sins are and see how different people and circumstances affect your ability to withstand those sins. You have to know how to live deeply by the heart instead of shallowly by the brain. It can seem overwhelming. That's why I do what I do.

Question: I don't suffer from greed, but sometimes I feel jealous when I see what other people are able to achieve because of their greed.

I used to be the same way. It wasn't exactly jealousy, though. I was more like Forrest Gump, looking around and not understanding what was wrong with me. Why wasn't I like everyone else? Why do other people feel driven to get ahead and I don't? I was perfectly happy with my own life, but I spent too much time wondering why I was so different. I even wondered if I should try and be like other people. It seemed like I'd never turn out to be much if I didn't have greed and ambition. After all, the negative traits we've talked about in this section of the book are the very things that help people succeed in society. But we've also seen how those same negative traits cut us off from our inner voices, from our hearts, and from God. Pride and greed are followed by fear and anger. The sins are the foundation for a soul-less, materialistic life.

Now, here's an interesting question: once you see how sin breaks you down, can you find a way to become successful without leveraging those negative traits that society encourages? The answer is yes: you can foster positive traits that give you strength and lead you to real success with honesty and kindness, without anger and fear. You can choose the path of darkness and live by sin and by instinct, and you may very well end up successful in the world's eyes. Or you could choose a more difficult path, weeding out your negative traits and building up positive traits that give you strength. And once you've done that, your positive traits will bring you material rewards.

People are always asking me how they can cleanse themselves of sin and still succeed in this life. That's how you do it: you become a good person and keep working on your positive traits. As those traits become stronger, you'll find you have more inspiration and healthy ambition than before. I've seen it work so many times. But we'll talk more about positive characteristics in the second half of this book. For now, we're focusing on the sins, which, if you remember, all start with pride. Once we're done talking about the sins, we'll look at the virtues and good deeds that make you stronger, and I'll explain how you can switch off all those sins and turn on your strengths to become kinder, fairer, and more honest. You'll be able to succeed in business and in life without being controlled by sin.

Question: I have friends who are always on the lookout for sales and discounts on things they want to buy. Is that a form of greed?

When I first started writing books and giving lectures, I noticed that the people who seem to have the worst luck, the people who seem like they're being punished for something, are the ones who spend the most time looking for discounts, sales, and coupons. People who are happy are also satisfied financially. They have what they want and want what they have, so they don't bother hunting for discounts online.

I'm not all what you would think of as a well-read or educated person, but I see how the world is designed and I see what happens when people follow that design or don't follow it. People are always asking me, "Why shouldn't I hunt for discounts?" "Why shouldn't I drink fresh-squeezed papaya juice?" or "Why shouldn't I wear hair extensions and acrylic nails?" The answer is because all those things come from sin, even if they look harmless on the outside. This book is where I lay it all out for you so you see where all the sins come from and what actions make it harder for you to get free of sin. And after that, I'll explain how you can turn on your positive, virtuous qualities.

When I started activating my positive qualities so they would shine, I used artefacts to reinforce those virtues. It's interesting how it all works. Once you activate your virtues, your whole life changes. It's like you're in a different movie all of a sudden. You turn off the red lights and turn on the green lights, and suddenly everything starts happening the way you want. You may be at the same job and with the same person, but everything makes sense and you experience joy like never before. So, keep reading.

Question: Where is the boundary between wanting to have nice things and becoming a greedy person?

You can feel the line. It's all about your intentions. Are you motivated by your self-doubt or your desire to show off in front of others? Do you want people to see how much money you have and what you buy with it? I have plenty of money, and I'd say I live pretty well, but keep a low profile because I don't want to provoke or tempt anyone. That's the first rule I developed for myself years ago: don't allow yourself to be provoked, and don't provoke others. Most people live on such low frequencies that they react instinctively to everything that happens around them, and I don't want to make anyone jealous. I'll never buy a Lamborghini and drive it around town slowly so that everyone sees me. I could buy one if I wanted to, but I'm not interested.

But here's a different scenario: I could buy a Land Rover with all the luxury options because I want to take a trip where there aren't any roads. I need an off-road vehicle, I like the features on the Land Rover, and I can afford to pay for it. Do you see the difference?

Most people buy expensive jewellery so they can show off. So, everyone will know how much money they have. I wear rings with precious stones because they have a positive effect on me. It's a little embarrassing. Here I am preaching minimalism and wearing expensive rings. But I have a reason that feeds the virtues in my life. Again, do you see the difference?

When you think about buying something to improve your quality of life, ask yourself what your motivations are. It may look like there is a thin line between living a good life and falling into greed, but when you examine your motivations, it's always absolutely clear. Don't be afraid of making yourself and your family comfortable, but also be aware of your true desires. If you're buying a house or an apartment, look for a nice neighbourhood with good schools and a public library instead of the trendiest neighbourhood with a yoga studio on every corner. If you're in the market for a new car, get something you enjoy driving that doesn't scream how much you spent for it. If you're buying clothes, go for quality. Get 100% cashmere if you want. But don't buy anything that has the name of the designer on it. Wear what makes you comfortable and happy, not what you think you need to wear to look better than everyone else.

Shallow people always spend money to make themselves look better, to cover up their insecurities. If you're in the market for a new car, a new home, or even just a vacation, ask yourself who you're doing it for. Did you know that there are people who take trips to exotic locations just so they can post the photos on Instagram? That's greed, and there's nothing entertaining about it. Instead, if you buy a new car, don't show it off to anyone. If you meet a movie star, don't post a selfie. If you spend your vacation on the most incredible tropical island, keep the memories for your own benefit.

I work with plenty of famous people, but I don't share photos. I don't even take photos. That's part of the agreement when I work with public figures, and it's one of the things that creates trust.

When you've worked hard to get rid of your sin and you're self-sufficient and happy, you're like a child playing with Lego bricks on the floor. The work you're doing absorbs all your attention, and you don't care if anyone is watching or not. But if you're still sinful, then you're worried about how many likes your Lego creation will get on Instagram. Because if you don't get enough likes, you don't exist. And you're competing against all the other kids posting photos of their Legos.

Here's an interesting example. The other day, I posted a bottle of whiskey I'd just bought on Instagram. Not to show off, but just so that people know I'm human. I enjoy a glass of whiskey every now and then. I used to drink 21-year Balvenie, but someone told me to try a 28-year Teeling, so that's the bottle I posted. Was I showing off? Not at all. A single bottle of whiskey, even the nice stuff, isn't a big purchase for me. My hope was that some of my loyal readers would remember the bottle and give it a try some time. Then we could compare notes.

Question: Do parents make their children greedy when they buy them expensive things?

That's a possibility, but there are a lot of factors at play. Children are born with their own souls, remember? The way a child is raised is certainly important, but you shouldn't worry about it too much. All the worrying you do as a parent (Am I giving my kid enough? Am I giving them too much?) does nothing but harm your child. And it doesn't help you, either. Choose what you believe to be right and do it. During the years that you raise a child, you're giving them yourself. All of your knowledge and all of your baggage. That's going to be your child's foundation in life. Once they're grown, they'll decide which of those things to keep and which to get rid of. That's perfectly normal. As long as your behaviour is ethical and kind, you don't need to worry about living up to anyone else's standard. If you want your child to be a vegetarian, you can do that. You have the right. Just don't be surprised if they grow up and decide to eat meat, because they have that right. It goes both ways.

I don't go around blaming parents for their children's sins. Each one of us was born into the family we deserve, and we take our knowledge and our material conditions from those families. Once we're grown, we choose which things to keep and which things to set down. That's how life works.

Question: Is it greed when a person scrimps and saves and never wants to spend money?

It's fine to be careful because you have to stick to a budget. Let's say I'm renovating my house. I'm not going to choose the most expensive marble floors made by hand by master craftsmen in Italy because then I wouldn't have any money left to pay for the rest of the work. So, those kinds of considerations—I like this, but can I afford it?—are absolutely normal.

Trying to save money only becomes a sin if you can't control it. If you always want the cheapest option because you have this animal instinct that pushes you that way, then that's greed. There have always been people that suffer from that particular form of greed. They buy shoes that they know are going to fall apart in a few months. They eat food they don't even like because it costs less.

Do you know what's best for you? The middle ground. Don't buy the most expensive bag: you might not be able to afford it, and you run the risk of feeding those sins that want you to show off. And don't buy the cheapest bag: you're just trying to feel better about yourself and how economical you are, but that cheap bag will end up in a landfill. So, when you economise, do it wisely. Don't go to extremes to save money, and don't let your efforts to cut costs make you angry at your friends and family. If you're shopping for a new pair of shoes and see options for $700, $120, and $60, buy the shoes for $120. Go for the middle. That's always the wisest course of action.

Question: I've heard you say that young people should find jobs that pay well while they figure out what their passion is. Aren't you encouraging them to be greedy? I don't see the difference.

Greed is an instinct. An emotion. Greed is when you want to get your hands on a lot of money no matter what. Taking a job that pays well is just being reasonable. Here's an example: let's say my love in life is collecting butterflies. I'm good at it, and I've published some articles in journals, but no one is offering me a job in the field. So, what do I do? I go job hunting. And I take the job that pays the most. Even if it's in a different field or with a company that no one has ever heard of. Because I'm not interested in the prestige, I just need to save up enough money for a trip to Africa so I can collect even more butterflies.

Have you ever met someone who was proud of working at a supposedly prestigious job that didn't pay well? I'm here to tell you that there's nothing morally upstanding about that. They're showing off when they name-drop about their company. They can't show off with money, so they show off with pride.

Don't choose a job because you want to show off. Choose a job that will pay for your needs and wants. That's the only reasonable path.

Question: I'm well off, but I don't feel like sharing my money with my grown children or other relatives. Does that make me a greedy person?

Greed is a feeling. If you get an emotional kick from not sharing with your relatives, then you're probably greedy. If, on the other hand, you have a reason for not giving money to specific people—maybe you're concerned that they'll use it for drugs or gambling or hurt themselves in some other way—then you're trying to do what's best for them by not giving them money. Your motive is what makes the difference. Examine your heart and find out what your true reasons are.

Question: Where does greed come from?

Like all the sins, greed comes from your mind when you compare yourself to others. A person who lives by their heart has their own inner world. They know who they really are. If you let your inner light go out, then your mind will take over and start comparing you and what you have to other people and what they have. That's how society tempts you.

For a lot of young people, college is the first time they have that experience of feeling jealous or envious. You hear other students talking about where their parents work, the vacations they take, the cars they drive. And if you don't have those things, you start to feel bad. You feel like shit. So, you skip meals for weeks until you can buy yourself the kicks that will make you feel better.

What's the difference between the young person who doesn't care about what other people have and the young person who lies awake at night wanting things they can't afford? It's their hearts. If it bothers you to be around people who have expensive things you can't afford, then you have sin in your heart. If that sin wasn't there, you would be free of desire and envy.

Question: Does greed make you lose your soul?

Every single time. The terrible price of greed is your soul. You sell your soul to get all the things you want. That's what I mean when I say that sinful people are led by their minds. They make decisions based on where they get the greatest material benefit. That's greed.

Question: Is it greedy to want to be famous?

Definitely. The need for attention is always sinful. All the social networks were designed to exploit your need for attention. They've built a virtual world where you can feed your sin faster than you ever could in real life.

But here's the paradox: just because a person is popular, that doesn't mean they're sinful. There could be all sorts of reasons and motivations behind their situation. Think of a researcher who never had any desire to be famous, but then they made an amazing discovery and the whole world knows their name.

People ask me how I ended up with so many followers or how I made so much money. I tell them the truth: those were never my goals. That's exactly why I've been successful. Reading books about how to get ahead in business and dreaming of buying your first Ferrari won't get you where you want to go. That's the road to hell. And poverty.

Question: Are greed and shame related?

People feel shame when they can't accept themselves the way they are, when they're playing a role to try to earn acceptance. I've never experienced shame, but so many people carry it around with them that I've always had lots of opportunities to study shame and how it works. When a person suffers from shame, they create an illusion of themselves as a good person and try to make everyone believe in it. Greedy people do the same thing: they use material goods to show off and make themselves look wealthier and more important than they really are.

Remember, it doesn't have anything to do with the size of your bank account. I have plenty of money, but I don't suffer from greed because I don't have any emotions about that money. The minute you start to worry or fixate on money or other material things, you're caught in the greed trap. And eventually greed gives birth to fear, and you start worrying that you'll lose what you have. That sounds pretty hopeless, doesn't it? You work so hard to make it, whatever 'it' means to you, and then you sit around worrying about losing it. But if you become successful because you love what you do, not because you're driven by greed, then you won't be afraid of that success going away. You won't have any negative emotions at all, because you'll be free.

Question: Can your financial situation suffer when you get rid of your greed? What about a person who became successful through greed and then had a change of heart? Will they see all that money evaporate?

Absolutely not. In fact, their financial situation only stands to improve as they grow their awareness and get rid of their greed. Just imagine: you already have financial wellbeing, and now you have spiritual well-being. You only stand to gain. Although getting rid of greed is like waking up from a bad dream: you might decide that you don't need a lot of the material things you've collected along the way. Your values will change. You won't need to splash out on a Bentley because your needs and wants will be more modest. Another important consideration is that you'll have better quality people around you. All of those factors will work together to make you even more successful than you were before.

Question: What about the desire for power—is that greed, too?

Yes, greed is what drives people to want power. It's all about the desire to stand above everyone else and dominate. The people who ought to have power are never the ones who actually want it. If you offer a modest person power, they're surprised. They don't think they deserve it. Greed, on the other hand, pushes people to have more than everyone else, and once they have more money, the next step is power. That desire to control others is always sinful.

Question: Is worrying about your possessions a form of greed?

You have to be careful about your relationship to material things. It's good to take care of the things you have, but you don't want to be so tied to your things that you cry when you crack your phone's screen or get mud on your sneakers.

If you feel strongly about your stuff, then keep an eye on yourself. Don't let yourself go overboard. If you're pure inside, then you won't be devastated if your car gets scratched or wrecked or even stolen. But as soon as you let greed and other sins get their claws in you, you'll be walking around scared of every mud puddle.

Here's another thing: it's bad for you to have so much stuff in your space that you can't feel free and peaceful. Keep your living space, your network of friends, and even your clothes clean and uncluttered.

I don't mean that you should never buy anything new. New clothes can make you feel fresh. They add years to your life. Just don't turn it into an obsession.

Question: I'm confused about when it's ok to intentionally make friends with successful people. You said it's wrong, but what if I'm just looking to reach a new level in my life and I need some good examples around me?

If you hang out with someone because he lets you ride in his sweet car, that's greed. If you go out of your way to be friends with someone because they'll pay for your drinks, that's greed. But not every intentional friendship is a bad thing. It's good when you search out people at a higher frequency because you want to improve your life. As always, the difference is your motivation. Greed pushes you to connect with people who can give you something: a lead on a job, an introduction to someone important. That's sinful and wrong. Personal growth leads you to seek out people you can learn from. See the difference?

Sometimes people tell me that they can't afford to socialise with people who are at a higher frequency. It's easy enough to have a beer with your friend from high school. You just sit around talking about women. No stress at all. Meeting new people at a higher level can be incredibly stressful. You have to dress up. You have to be ready for a higher level of conversation. There's no greed at play here. You're paying your own way and investing in your future because you want to spend time on a higher frequency with people who think and read and talk about more than their exes or where they bought their shoes. Or maybe you're looking for professional contacts who are really doing something, making a difference, not just complaining about the industry. That's not greed. That's smart.

You can always check yourself by tuning in to your emotions. If you're dying to meet someone, that's a sign for caution. Greed is an animal instinct that drives you. Let's go back to my example with the handmade coffee mugs. If I'm desperate to meet with the buyer for a home goods store, then I'm being controlled by greed. If, on the other hand, I'm looking forward to showing off my mugs but I'm not emotionally tied to the outcome, then it's just business.

When bloggers and influencers throw parties, they don't invite the people they're truly close to. They message the people who have connections or money or followers. Better yet, all three. They want to make sure that the right people post photos from the party. That's a sign of pride and envy, but there's also some greed mixed in, because they want to benefit from being seen with the right people. They want to gain something.

My life doesn't work like that. When I invite people to my retreat in Karelia, I'm not putting together a list of people who can help me sell more books or consultations. I don't care who you know or how much money you have; if your sin controls you, I won't invite you. I'm looking for people who enjoy nature and will have a good time. That's all.

When people ask me, "What about this kind of business?" or "What about that kind of business?" I start to worry that they're missing the point. One person might open what looks like a socially responsible business but be driven by greed, while another person might start loaning venture capital and not be greedy at all.

Here's another way to check yourself: are you following your own ideas, or are you copying everyone else? If you're chasing after the latest business trend in hopes that it will make you rich like it did for someone you saw on social media, then that's your greed controlling you.

Question: Is it harder to get rid of your greed when you're already wealthy?

Remember that greed is an instinct, not a bank balance. There are greedy people in every tax bracket. If you do things that reinforce your greed, then it will get stronger. If you act on good intentions, your greed will get weaker. It's really that simple.

Question: What about a person who just wants to have a lot of money so they can live well and use it to do good, not because they want to show off?

A lot of people will tell you they don't want money for themselves, they want it so they can do good for the world. They do their greedy deeds in secret and then they turn around and tell you how much they love all the little children. I don't read minds exactly, but I can tell when people are lying about their intentions. When one of my consulting clients tells me that they want to make a lot of money so that they can do good works, not so they can spend it on sinful entertainment, I tell that client that they're deluding themselves. They can say anything they want, but their emotions tell the true story.

Don't be fooled by greedy people who say all the right things. They talk about making money so they can do good, or so they can further their education. But what they really want is money and power to satisfy their greed.

When people describe their goals in terms of money, that's already a problem. Goals have to grow from a better, deeper place than the desire for money. Here's a basic example. Let's say I want to learn to play the guitar. I go online and start looking for used guitars, and I message my friends to see if anyone has one they could sell me. But nobody has anything, so I head down to the guitar store, where the salesperson tells me I'll need to spend $450 to buy a basic guitar. If I don't have the money, I'll go look for a side hustle so I can make the money.

Do you see the difference? My goal was not to make money. My goal was to learn to play the guitar. I just realised along the way that I'd need some extra money to make that happen.

I see so many people who say they want to make money so they can improve themselves and do better in life, but when I ask them about their plans, their faces go blank. They don't have a plan. The truth is, they just want money without even knowing why. If you want something in life—whether it's a medical degree or a new pair of shoes—find out how much it costs and then look for opportunities to make that money. Always keep it specific. Figure out what you need to buy and do the work you're qualified to do so you can get yourself there.

Question: Is it greedy to be a collector of things like antiques?

It depends on *why* you're collecting, not the specific things you collect. Greed is a feeling. You might be a greedy person who collects cars to flex in front of your friends or collects antique clocks to keep other history buffs from getting their hands on them. But you might be a perfectly normal person collecting things you're interested in. Maybe you inherited a collection from your grandfather and you enjoy reading up on history and want to keep the collection going. That's not greed.

When you're wondering if you ought to do something or not, don't look at the externalities. Is it okay to spend this much on a car? Is it okay to take this job? Instead, look at your feelings and motivations. Are you buying the car because it fits your needs and you like it? Or are you buying it to send a message to everyone in the neighbourhood? Do you play golf because you love being outside in the sunshine and walking around the course? Or are you there so you can post photos of your new argyle vest? The problem isn't golf. The problem is you.

The same thing happens in relationships. A greedy person will choose to be with you for your connections, your money, your clothes. You're just a means to an end they want to achieve for themselves. A lustful person will want to be with you for your body. It isn't about you—it's about them. If you want to find true love, first you have to get rid of the seven deadly sins so you can let love in.

Being aware of your feelings is the best way to make sure you're making life choices with your virtues instead of your sins. When you have mixed emotions about a new relationship, that's the conflict between your virtuous side and your sinful side. Each of them is reacting to the new person in your life, and you have to learn which side to listen to.

Have you ever noticed how when you listen to music that makes you happy, maybe something you've loved since you were a kid, you'll suddenly start thinking about all the good friends you haven't hung out with in a long time? You think, "I need to find out how they're doing. Maybe we can hang out." There's even a hint in your mind that you might have more than a platonic interest in one of those friends. But then the next day you go to work and you're so busy, you skip lunch. You have a bunch of meetings where you have to pretend to care what's going on. By the end of the day, you don't want to see your old friends anymore. They don't seem important anymore. That's because you're looking at them through the sinful side of your personality that gets strengthened when you're at work.

So, you end up choosing a partner when your sinful side is strong. Everything seems great, but one day your soul wakes up and you roll over and look at your partner and your heart sinks. You think, "What have I done? I've tied myself to a person who isn't following their heart." This happens all the time, not only with huge, life-altering choices. You buy a car when your greed is strong. You take a job when you're feeling driven by pride. That's why I wanted to digress here. I want you to see how any choice you make can go either way. The sin isn't in the car or the job or the significant other. If there is any sin, it's in your motivation. Returning to the question, there's nothing wrong with collecting things you have a true interest in. It only becomes a problem if your motivations are greedy.

I hope you've done some deep thinking about all the sins from pride to greed that we've talked about so far. Are you starting to understand how the problem is always your reaction to a situation, not the situation itself? If so, that's good. Now we're going to talk about the last sin, despair. Then we'll move on to look at some other lower-level negative traits that don't make the list of top sins but can still get in your way on your journey toward personal growth. After that, we'll turn the corner and jump with both feet into the virtues and learn how you can feed your soul in wonderful ways.

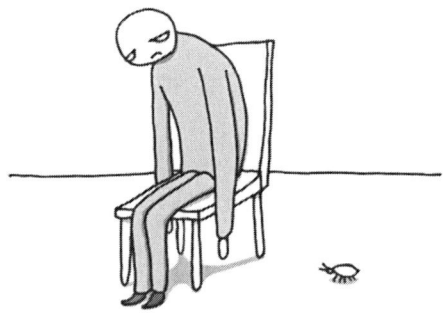

Despair

Take some time to write down how you understand the word 'despair.' What does it mean? Do you have any personal experience with despair? If so, write about that, too. Be sure to keep in mind all those stories from your past as you read through this section.

I bet you're wondering how despair could possibly be a sin. Everyone's in a bad mood sometimes, right? Are we sinning every time we get up on the wrong side of the bed? Absolutely not: despair is not the same as having a bad mood. It isn't the same as being depressed. Depression is a medical diagnosis. Despair is a spiritual state where you see everything negatively. You have no faith, because you don't believe in God; you have no hope because you don't believe in yourself; and you have no love because you reject the people around you.

When you give in to despair, you listen to your mind, and your mind tells you that everything around you is bad. That's why it's a sin—you're listening to your mind and letting your mind lead you instead of being led by faith.

Despair is a complicated topic, isn't it? The other sins are more obvious. At least, it's clear how people end up being driven by those sins. I have to admit that this was the hardest sin for me to think about when I was preparing to write this book. I have a hard time seeing how anyone could fall prey to despair. The people I've helped out of despair were all on a bad frequency that turned them away from the world. Not in the good sense of tuning out the world and tuning in to their hearts and their creativity, but in this very damaging, negative way. That frequency keeps people from seeing everything that's wonderful in the world. It's like they become blind. But despair doesn't come out of nowhere. I've noticed that the people who surround themselves with negative, pessimistic friends, listen to violent music, and watch violent movies are far more likely to fall prey to despair. Drugs and alcohol make it worse, too. Despair is a hole you dig for yourself.

The other sins may not satisfy your heart, but they satisfy your mind, at least for a while. A greedy person feels great when they buy something that nobody else in their friend group has. A prideful person experiences a temporary high when they post photos from their vacation in Bora Bora to social media. But despair is different. It doesn't even offer temporary pleasure. I believe that despair catches up with us when we've gone so far away from what our hearts truly desire that even our minds are burned out. When you despair, you feel worthless.

Like all the other sins, despair describes what's in your heart, not the situation or people around you. A healthy person can lose a competition or see their start-up fold after six months and still not despair, because they have a fire inside. They have their faith intact. But when a soul-less, materialistic person fails to achieve their goals, they fall into despair.

Here's an interesting fact: some translations call the sin of losing hope 'despair,' but other translations call it 'sloth,' or laziness. Somehow those two concepts are tied together, and we're going to consider them together.

If you look at this sin from the sloth angle, you see a person who's lost their reason for living. Maybe you used to have a fire inside, but the fire went out and you're left with nothing but sins to motivate you. So, you just shrug and let everything go. School, work, friendships, romantic relationships: you let it all slide. Despair is an energy suck. It makes you lazy.

For the past ten years, all kinds of people have asked me where I get my inspiration from. Where do I find the energy to take up new hobbies while running a business and writing books? My answer is that it all comes from inside me. The positive qualities I've tried to feed all my life are the very virtues we're going to be talking about in the second half of this book. If I lost my creative drive all of a sudden, I'd have to look in my heart for the sin that took it away.

The sins and virtues are like different parts of a computer program. Once you understand how the human heart works, you can turn the creative flow on or turn it off. That explains why so many people have one big success and then burn out. They write one great book or make one great movie, and then they fall prey to sin, lose their inspiration, and never really make anything worthwhile for the rest of their lives.

So many people are used to leveraging their sin as a motivator. Feeling bad about themselves is what pushes them to look good in the world's eyes. But other people are motivated by their virtues, instead. Paradoxically, when virtuous people fail at something, they don't have sinful pride or envy or greed to fall back on, and they, too, can sink into despair.

Resentment is another pathway that leads to despair, as is greed. When you feel like you don't have something you ought to have, something you see other people enjoying, you're allowing your mind to take control. Your mind sees that you're a failure, so it starts telling you, you're worthless. That deep, wounding disappointment snuffs out your inner fire and drags you into a place of despair. You may still be alive physically, but your spirit is dead. I've seen this so many times.

Again, I want you to notice that all the sins are connected, and all of them come from the mind. This is critical: if you allow your mind to desire something and then you lose that thing, you'll fall straight into despair. One example of this would be falling in love with a person, but only with your mind, not your heart. Then, if that person doesn't reciprocate, you end up in an emotional tailspin because your mind didn't get what it wanted. Likewise, if you allow your mind to define your goals and fail to achieve those goals, you'll start to despair. Those are the two pathways to despair that I've seen.

Questions and Answers about Despair

Question: I had a goal that I was excited about, but I ended up changing my focus and working toward something else. My friend says I'm lazy for not finishing the first thing I started. Is that true?

Possibly. I can think of a number of reasons why you might not finish something you started. Laziness, or sloth, which is just one specific kind of despair, can show up in our lives in a couple of different ways. The first type of sloth trips you up when you are always going with the flow and following other people. People who just stand back and let life run its course tend to encounter the same kinds of problems over and over, and one of those is failing to follow through on plans. Why does this happen? Because the goals you're working toward don't come from your heart. They may come from your parents or your friends or social media, but they don't reflect your true wishes. You may start working toward your goals, but you can't force yourself to follow through.

That's a chaotic way to live. Maybe you hang out with your friends one weekend and go home with this idea that you'll move to the country and raise chickens. But after a couple of days, you start listening to the wrong music or watching the wrong movies and you forget all about the plan to raise chickens. Then the next week it's some other plan.

Once you start working on your inner self, however, the chaos goes away and you start to understand what you really want to achieve. That's a powerful change, because once your goals are aligned with your heart, the work of achieving those goals makes you stronger. You won't forget what you wanted or get distracted by other people's ideas about what you should do.

The other way I see sloth hold people back is when they let their mood run the show. Maybe you have a great idea for a new business, but you wake up on the wrong side of the bed and decide to watch Netflix instead of sketching out a business plan. "Later," you think. "I can do that later when I feel like it." That's absolutely sloth.

This happens to people who aren't used to the rhythm of work. Hard work is easy to learn when we're small children, but it gets harder to learn to work the older we are. If you grew up with this illusion that life is supposed to be easy, then the temptation of sin will always be stronger than the potential future pays out of hard work. You're used to being able to hang out and do what you want when you want, so as soon as your project or plan runs into an obstacle, you just give up. People usually blame their circumstances for this kind of failure: "I didn't have the capital or the knowledge I needed at the right time." How often have you heard excuses like that? I know I've heard them a million times. But that's not what happened. It was laziness.

Imagine you want something that is going to take some effort over time to achieve. It could be anything. Maybe you want to start a side hustle to make some extra cash. Or you come up with a sweet idea for painting a mural on your bedroom wall. But when you get started, you realise that you'll have to work harder than you're used to working. So, you let it slide. You give up.

This kind of sloth can damage relationships, too. I usually see it in people who have been single for years and years. They have these fixed habits that they aren't willing to change, and once they start living with another person, they feel uncomfortable. They just can't adapt.

But I don't want to digress too much on the topic of relationships here, because my focus is on sloth and how it affects your ability to follow through on plans. Don't make excuses for why you can't achieve something. If your goal is to offer custom tailoring but you can't find the fabrics you want, look for a supplier in Italy. Or go there yourself. Or use something else. Just don't tell me you can't start your custom tailoring business because the right fabric didn't fall in your lap. That's laziness. If your goal is to meditate every day, don't wait for the mood to strike you. Just sit down and meditate. Maybe you want to write a book, but you keep waiting for the right time to get started. Here's a hint: there is no right time—you just have to open your laptop and get started.

Get used to doing what needs to be done, even if that means changing your mood. I can hang out with my friends all morning, taking photos and listening to music, and then go back to my home office and work through serious meetings where I have to focus on details and take notes. I can go back and forth from dreamer mode to worker mode. That's hard for a lot of people to do, because they think that dreaming and working are *moods* that strike out of the blue. I'm here to tell you that's nonsense. Dreaming and working are *modes* that you have to turn on for yourself.

If you want the strength to achieve your goal—whether it's writing a book, or painting a mural, or starting a business—you have to let go of the sin of despair or sloth. The perfect time to get started is now.

Question: What causes despair in children? I understand how an adult could fall into despair because of negative experiences in their life, but what about a child?

Despair in children is always caused by the adults around them. Your kid needs you, but whenever the two of you talk, it always turns into an argument. So, they stop sharing their burdens with you. Do you see how that could cause despair in a child? Kids who grow up in families that listen to them without judgement share more. Don't get me wrong: my parents were strict. We didn't have a television to watch cartoons, and I never had a computer. But I had plenty of books and art supplies, and I felt seen and heard. My parents also never gave me an allowance. I don't think I ever had money in my pocket until I started working. And you know what? It didn't matter. I was always a dreamer, and my family was supportive of that. Providing that kind of love and support is so much more important than any money you might spend on your child's activities or buying them things.

One thing I loved doing on my own as a kid was raising rabbits to sell. My parents gave me the freedom to do that, and they were proud of the work I put into it. They didn't run out and buy me a lot of supplies for keeping rabbits. They just made sure I had the basics and kept an eye on me. When your child shows an interest in something, treat that interest with respect and be supportive. It's all too easy to be dismissive, but your child's passions and the microbusinesses they launch—the lemonade stand, the friendship bracelets, the YouTube channel—show you who they are and who they'll be when they grow up.

A lot of parents fall into the opposite mistake of trying to force their kids to be interested in things. Imagine what it feels like to have to work at something you don't love because you need your parents' approval. And then when it doesn't work out—you don't make the team, or you never get good at the skill they wanted you to have—you experience this deep disappointment that can turn into despair. You have to let your children figure out what they're good at and get behind them.

Question: Why do some people choose to sit around and do nothing with their lives?

Laziness has two parts: first of all, lazy people don't want to exert themselves; and second, they don't have the fire inside that would make them want to get up and do something.

Sin fuels that desire to do nothing. But when you have the inner fire that comes from the soul, you can't lie around in despair. You naturally want to achieve things and get things done. Once you get a handle on your sins, suddenly you look around and see all these interesting things you could be doing. I love to see that happen for people.

Question: Is despair just a bad mood that comes and goes?

Not exactly. Despair is something you bring on yourself. It's when you have a negative attitude every day. You have a distorted view of your life because your sins are strong and you aren't feeding your soul. Feeling blue when you have a specific reason for that feeling is not the same as ongoing despair.

Question: Some of my relatives are negative all the time. Is it wrong of me to avoid them?

Not at all. People with more traditional views of the family might disagree with me, but I don't believe in being masochistic. I don't want to become negative, so I stay away from negative people. Respecting your elders is a virtue, but that doesn't mean you have to subject yourself to someone else's despair. You can reach out sometimes and see if they want to take a walk or go to a movie with you, but if they persist in being negative, then you have every reason to walk away.

There's no moral law that says you have to lower yourself to your family member's frequency. If they want to be angry and despairing, that's their choice. This is especially true if your family member's despair takes the form of drug or alcohol abuse. You can reach out and say, "I love you, here's what I'm prepared to do for you to help you get back on your feet." But if they persist in using their substance of choice, cut them off and don't look back. They made their choice. Nobody's asking them to get clean without help. We all know that's impossible. But if they won't even take the help that's offered, then they can deal with the consequences of their actions. No amount of heroism on your part will help.

Here's another way to think of it: when you keep rescuing a person who is in despair, you're feeding that despair. You're helping them stay stuck. So, don't do it. Don't let them suck the life out of you. You can't help them, and you'll only hurt yourself.

Question: Is despair the same as being in the Corridor?

Not at all. In fact, they're the opposite. Let me explain what the Corridor is for anyone who hasn't read my first book. The Corridor is where you are when your mind is turned off. It's a meditative state where your sins and animal instincts are dormant. You're in the corridor between worlds. You realise that the material world is an illusion, and your soul starts to open up. You can finally see the people living in other worlds at other frequencies. A person in the Corridor is quiet and introspective, but definitely not despairing. Quite the opposite, despair is created by an overactive mind. You sit around listening to sad music and not doing anything. Some people think that they're meditating when they're actually just sitting around in despair. The difference may not be obvious from the outside, but a person in the Corridor is making their way toward something better. They aren't stuck in the negativity of despair.

Question: Can losing someone close to you make you despair?

It depends on the relationship. If I lose someone I was connected to by my heart, then I won't fall into despair. I'll let them go, but my soul will grow even larger with the love that we shared. I'll become wiser and stronger in spirit. But if I was connected to the person through my mind, then the relationship is like an addiction. Shallow relationships keep you in your comfort zone, and when you suddenly lose that person, your comfort zone is gone. You're lost. You despair.

I'm discovering new things all through this process of writing about despair and answering people's questions. It's helping me organise my thoughts. I've realised that all of the other sins—anger, gluttony, pride—eventually lead to despair. If you're letting sin rule some area of your life, that turns on all the other sins, including despair.

Question: How can I help myself out of despair?

You need to understand the virtues before you can get rid of your sin. Once despair has you in its clutches, you can't just pull yourself up by your bootstraps. You can't force yourself to feel love, or inspiration, or a desire to accomplish something. It doesn't work that way. The first step is to stop feeding your belief that you're worthless. You do that by getting rid of certain kinds of negative factors in your life. I'm going to talk about that in more detail later. For now, I'll just say that none of my recommendations cost anything. You don't even have to work hard at it. All you have to do is accept some restrictions that will stop feeding your sins. Fasting is just one example of the kinds of restrictions I recommend. Once you accept the restrictions, your despair will begin to fade. That's the short explanation.

That leads me back to a question a lot of people ask me: "How do I know if I want something with my heart or my mind?" It's a question that is top-of-mind for everybody. Here's the answer: you don't have to figure it out. If you just read along through the book, even if you only understand 20-30% of it, you'll start to make better choices. If you pick up a few things that you need to stop doing and a few things that you ought to be doing, and you follow through on that, you're already on your way to improving your life. The process is like taking vitamins. You don't need to understand why they work in order for them to work. Once you start following even just a few of my suggestions, you'll notice that your desires change. Your relationships will be more fulfilling, and your work will be more rewarding. Turning your life around is not about understanding everything with your mind; instead, it's about tuning into your heart and choosing things that support your heart.

Now that you have a basic understanding of the sins and how they hurt you, we're going to talk about virtues and how they help you. In the second half of this book, you'll be focused on positive traits and finding them in yourself. You'll notice that you start having better, kinder thoughts. It happens on its own. You may find that you're drawn to hang out with a different group of people than before you read this book. Your old friends—the ones who complain about everything, who love to blame everyone around them—don't appeal to you anymore. So, you start hanging out with positive people who may have been in your life before, but you were never that close to them. That, my friends, is growth.

Question: It sounds like all the other sins motivate you to do things, even if it's the wrong things, while despair keeps you stuck in one place. Why is despair so different?

That's what it looks like on the surface, but remember, despair boils down to this: having a negative attitude toward everything. You can be in despair and still live your life, going to work, coming home, making dinner. But you don't enjoy any of it. You don't love your life, or yourself, or God, and you become a source of temptation for others, driving them into sin. It works just like a virus.

Our job is to learn where the pitfalls are and free our souls from sin. Then we become aliens in the world of sin and start working to free others. That's the path to personal growth.

Question: When I'm critical of myself, is that the sin of despair?

Most definitely. Self-criticism comes from viewing yourself—and everyone else—through the prism of negativity that despair holds up. People who hate others hate themselves, too. That's where self-criticism comes in. Being in despair doesn't mean you're necessarily sitting on your bed and staring off into space. That's what it looks like for some people, but we can't generalise that image to everyone. There are plenty of despairing people who don't fit that stereotype.

A despairing person might be active physically and active at work, but nothing suits them. They think their co-workers, their partner, and their parents are all full of shit. God is full of shit. Everything is awful. For these people, despair doesn't look like sloth. It's just total negativity.

Despair is definitely more complex than the other sins. The easiest way to understand it is like this: despair means being negative about everything. That negativity might make you lazy and slow to act, but it also might make you really angry and even violent. Your eyes work like a mirror: if you have love in your heart, you see the world through that love. If your heart is despairing, then nothing measures up. Everything looks bad and wrong and awful. Including yourself.

Question: I picked up your book because a friend recommended it to me. But here's the catch: my friend leads a really sinful life. That makes me wonder if your advice really works.

Does a person become a saint when they buy one of my books? I doubt it. But I'm glad to hear about your friend. They may not have made changes in their life yet, but something is waking up in their heart. But that doesn't mean you should follow their example. Anyone is free to read my books, even murderers. I've received letters from readers who are in prison. Not everyone takes the straight and narrow path to living an enlightened life. Plenty of people read my books and then go right back to being driven by gluttony and pride. All I can do is hold up a mirror to your life and ask you to look in it.

If you meet someone who goes to church every week and says they believe in God, does that mean they live a perfect life without sin? Of course not. Churches are full of prideful, angry, envious people.

Spiritual growth has become trendy, and that's a shame. A lot of the options out there aren't worth anything. Do you follow along with a meditation app while you walk on the treadmill at the gym? Well, I have news for you: that isn't really meditation. Do you light incense when you feel stressed out? It may smell nice, but it won't help. People keep buying material solutions to spiritual problems, and it doesn't work that way.

The only way to really grow spiritually is to first take a hard look at yourself and your soul. I've had a few readers write to me and say that they feel like they have a heavier burden of sin after they read my books. What's really happening is that they have a clearer view of the sin that was already there. That's a good first step. There's nothing wrong with feeling disgusted by the sin you see when you examine your soul. Once you've seen virtue, sin looks even blacker.

Negative Traits

Before we look at the virtues, I want to show you a list of negative characteristics that aren't deadly sins, and yet they affect a lot of people's lives. These are characteristics that feed sin and are fed by sin. I compiled the list below from questions my readers have sent in. Some of the items in the list will surprise you, but remember: for each item, there is someone out there who feels like this trait is a problem in their life.

- Adultery
- Aggression
- Anxiety
- Apathy
- Arrogance
- Blasphemy
- Boastfulness
- Callousness
- Carelessness
- Complaining
- Cravings
- Cruelty

Dependency
Desire for power
Egoism
Flattery
Forgetfulness
Gloating
Head in the clouds
Hypocrisy
Immaturity
Indecisiveness
Ingratitude
Jealousy
Joking
Keeping a dirty house
Lack of faith
Laziness
Low self-esteem
Narcissism
Not caring about anyone
Offensiveness
Oversleeping
Pettiness
Physical abuse
Pushiness
Rudeness
Short temper
Slander
Stealing
Strategizing
Stubbornness
Stupidity
Taking bribes
Taking offense
Talking too much
Telling lies
Thoughtlessness

Vulgarity
Wanting revenge
Wasting time

Here are my quick takes on a handful of these:

Did you see **joking** in the list and wonder why it was there? Humour is pretty harmless, right? I like to joke around with friends. But the intention behind the humour is what matters. Don't hurt people's feelings or use your humour to cover up what's really a humble brag.

Strategizing is another one that some might find surprising. After all, we're supposed to make plans and follow through. But there is good strategizing and bad strategizing. If you tell lies to pursue your strategy, that becomes a problem. Again, your intention is what matters. If I invite my team to spend a week of vacation with me at a resort and don't tell them that a famous rock star is going to be there at the same time, I didn't lie by omission because I wanted to gain something for myself. I left out that information because I don't want it to influence my team members. I only want them to come on the trip if they really want to spend time with me. So, I'm strategizing, but for a kind, good purpose.

Bad strategizing involves lying or omitting information for personal gain. Imagine that a contractor quotes you $5,000 to build a home office in your backyard. That's less than you expected, so you're happy with the quote and ready to write a check. But then you look at the contract and see another several thousand in fees and add-ons that they didn't mention.

Carelessness seems harmless enough. After all, when I'm careless, I'm the only one who suffers the consequences, right? Unfortunately, that really isn't the case. If someone pays you to do a job and you don't do it right, the customer suffers. If you're months late finishing a project, your team members and your employer suffer. We're supposed to treat our tasks and the people around us with care and attention.

Boastfulness is always a problem, but it can be caused by different types of sin. A boastful person might lack confidence or suffer from pride or greed. It's all interconnected.

When you **slander** someone, you say critical things about them that aren't true. You're slinging mud at that person to hurt their reputation, lying to make others turn away from them. Slander has always been a problem, and social media has just made it worse. Now, there are more people with public reputations and more people looking to take them down. Why would someone engage in slander? Possibly because they're greedy and hope to benefit from their rival's downfall. This type of greed usually goes hand in hand with anger. Despair might also be in the mix.

Rude people take what they want without asking. They don't respect other people's comfort zones. They suffer from egoism that is fed by any of the deadly sins.

This list should make a lot more sense now that we've talked about each of the seven deadly sins. You have all the context you need to look at the negative characteristics in the list and see them for what they are: either the seeds or the fruit of the deadly sins. If the deadly sins are too abstract for you, just focus on these negative characteristics. Getting rid of even some of them will help you cleanse your heart of sin. Remember: every time you lose your temper and fight with your family or do a sloppy job at work, you're feeding one of the deadly sins. And when you work hard on removing one of these negative traits from your life, the others will start to weaken, too.

The Ten Commandments

- You shall have no other gods before me.
- You shall not make for yourself an idol in the form of anything in heaven above or on the earth beneath or in the waters below.
- You shall not misuse the name of the Lord your God.
- Six days you shall labour and do all your work, but the seventh day is a Sabbath to the Lord your God. On it, you shall not do any work.
- Honour your father and your mother.
- You shall not murder.
- You shall not commit adultery.
- You shall not steal.
- You shall not give false testimony against your neighbour.
- You shall not covet your neighbour's house or his wife.

Let's take a look at the Ten Commandments before we move on to the virtues.

"You shall have no other gods before me." That means that there is one God. There can't be any others.

"Don't make idols." Focus on God. Making an idol doesn't always mean creating a god-like statue out of gold or bronze and bowing down to it. Anyone you're attached to can become your idol. Any time your attention is more focused on a person in your life than on God, that person is your idol. You've created an idol. Remember that there is always something greater than your human life, and stay plugged in to that knowledge. Because God is greater and more powerful than anything you can imagine. When you let yourself become mesmerised by a person, whether it's someone you're in love with or an artist or businessperson you have great admiration for, that means you're turning your face away from God.

"Don't misuse God's name." If you call out to God with a pure heart, he hears you. That's not something to take lightly. Whenever you call out his name, be aware of what you are connecting to. He can hear you. Don't speak his name unless you need him.

"Work six days and rest on the seventh." Even before I'd read the Bible, I was telling people that everyone should take a day off each week to rest and recharge. Why should you make rest a priority? Because when you're involved in work and socialising, you get tuned to the people around you. You need to spend a day alone to cleanse your heart and strengthen your connection to God. That day doesn't have to fall on Sunday. You could choose Friday or Saturday or any other day. But it has to be a whole 24 hours for meditating. No phone, no friends, just you and God.

"Honour your father and mother." This simple phrase is the foundation of how God wants us to approach the world around us. Our parents are the first people we know. Your father is the first man you meet, and your mother is the first woman you meet. They're different from you, and you're different from them. God wants us to accept our parents, because that makes us better able to accept the other people we meet as we go through life. He doesn't want us to get hung up on how we're different from our parents or how they don't understand us. We're just supposed to love and accept them. When you can do that, you cleanse a lot of the anger, aggression, and resentment from your heart, and you'll also be able to find common ground with anyone you meet. This commandment reminds us that the journey of acceptance starts at home.

"Do not murder." This one should be obvious. If you commit murder, you create the ultimate idol—your own power—and you sever your relationship to God. The light in your heart goes off.

"Do not commit adultery." You already understand that all the sins are interconnected. Adultery is like lying or stealing in that it weakens your heart and takes you away from God. When your heart is pure, you can find joy in petting a dog or taking a hike or watching the sun set. Actions like adultery and lying suck the joy and meaning right out of your life.

Readers' Questions and Answers

Why do people take communion and then go out and continue sinning?

Communion wine doesn't change your heart any more than wearing a cross around your neck or listening to Christian music would. That's a naive way to think about morality. Remember, I studied math at college. I can tell you for a fact that there is no such thing as miracles. All that happens when you go to church and listen to the music is that the power of your mind lessens and your negative, sinful traits are weakened. Your heart starts to wake up a little bit. The strength of the effect depends on the person.

Imagine that I live with a bunch of drug addicts who fund their addiction by packaging and selling fentanyl. They're driven by greed and gluttony. They listen to angry music. That's the negative environment I live in. Now imagine that I go to church. And I don't stop there. I go to a bunch of different churches. I even go visit some Tibetan monks. And all of those experiences clean my heart up. I leave feeling a thousand times better. I'm 100% recharged. But as soon as I get a message from one of my junkie roommates, all the positive effects are gone. My body and my nervous system remember the filth I live in. It hasn't gone anywhere.

Do you see why I'm always telling people that it matters what kind of music you listen to and what kind of movies you watch? It matters what you eat and who you socialise with. You can end up drowning because of one single person. Even if you haven't seen them in ages. Just by texting or chatting. So, be mindful of who you allow into your life.

When people read your books or listen to your talks, do they connect to your frequency?

That's basically how it works. I wrote my first book, *Paradox*, to turn down people's minds and turn up their hearts. I wanted my readers who were already living by their hearts to experience greater joy and inspiration, and I wanted my readers who were still living in sin to see that sin clearly and realize the filth they had taken on. I wanted them to be shocked enough that they would start to turn things around.

Life is divided into the sinful and the spiritual. I'm not the only one who can be like a wi-fi router and connect people to the spiritual world. Anyone can do it. If I have five spiritually centred people in my life, then I will become even more spiritual. But if I have five sinful people around me, their sin will stick to me and I'll eventually become like them. That's how it works. We all influence each other more than we realise, and those of us with strong sins or strong virtues pull the others along with us.

I'm describing it in simple terms, but the mechanism by which we influence each other is complex and powerful. Say, you live in a city where most of the people are greedy and aggressive. No matter how kind and generous you are, the greed and aggression around you will rub off on you. Frequencies are powerful, and you don't have to understand how they work to see that they *do* work.

I feel like I do a good job of honouring my parents. I accept them the way they are, without any anger or resentment. But whenever they call me, I feel out of sorts for days afterwards. How can I have a relationship with them? I don't want to cut them off, but I also don't like how they make me feel.

I understand what you're saying. Some parents are hard to deal with, especially as they get older. But this is part of life. Just as you had to fall off your bike and skin your knees when you were a kid, now at this stage of life you have to learn to handle your parents and their needs. You'll care for your parents, and someday you'll bury them, just as your children will care for you and bury you. That's the circle of life. If you can learn to look at it this way, your faith will be stronger and your fears will grow smaller. The more you understand, the less afraid you are.

But what can you do to feel better about the relationship right now? First, you have to understand that there's a weakness in you somewhere if talking to your parents upsets you. That weakness doesn't necessarily come from sin, but it's fed by negative traits that you need to pay attention to. And it also means that you need to activate your virtues. The light inside you is faint and tired. Once you learn how to turn on the seven virtues, your soul will grow stronger and your nervous system will be so steady that nothing your parents say can hurt you.

You'll be able to talk to them without experiencing any of the negative emotions that are upsetting you now.

Why do some people's consciences keep them away from temptation, while other people's don't?

This is a great question to end this section of the book with, because the answer gets at the root of everything. Here are some examples that will help you understand the answer.

The first example is twin brothers living in the same family. They have all the same things, and their parents treat them the same. Their parents teach both of them the commandments: don't lie, don't steal, don't kill. One of the brothers understands the commandments and follows them. The other brother breaks every rule he's been given. They were raised the same, but one understood and the other didn't. Why does that happen? Because when we're born, our souls are born along with us. We're born into families. They give us our names. They give us our nationalities. But we bring our souls with us. Some people have deep, wise souls, and others have thin, hungry souls. Think of a baby's soul as its life experience. One of the boys learned in a previous life that he didn't want to live in sin. He was born already knowing the code. The other boy was born without that experience, and his parents' moral teaching just goes in one ear and out the other. So, the first part of my explanation as to why one person has a conscience that keeps them from temptation and another person doesn't is all about nature. The second part of my explanation is about nurture—how you nurture your soul. If you are spiritually pure, you won't be able to steal or sell drugs or commit adultery. You couldn't do it even if someone begged you. When I say that's due to nurture, I'm not talking about how your parents raised you. I'm talking about how you take care of your own soul. That's the most important lesson I want you to take away from this section. You can choose to neglect your soul or choose to nurture it. You can let the seven virtues be your seven guiding lights

A Final Word

We've reached the end of our study of humankind's greatest problems—the seven deadly sins. These are the negative traits, or animal instincts, that feed your mind while starving your heart. I'm grateful that my book found its way into your hands, and if you feel it's helped you look at your life a little differently, I hope you'll look me up on social media and let me know. And one last thing: don't give up. Use my simple explanations to avoid temptation. Surround yourself with good people. And let the fire inside you burn brightly!

In the first volume, I showed you the seven animal instincts in the human mind, also known as the seven deadly sins. In this volume, I'll show you the seven positive qualities of the human soul, also called the seven virtues. Love is the most important of the virtues, because love is acceptance without anger or anxiety.

Alexandr Korol

Volume Two: Virtues

Introduction

Like most people, I grew up hearing the word 'virtue' but not really knowing what it meant. I'm not an academic, and I think that's one of the things that attracts people to the information I share. There are plenty of shallow people out there who know all the words and terms without understanding the deepest truths. I'm more interested in that truth, and I hope you are, too.

In the first volume of this book, we looked at the dark side of the soul: sins and negative traits that make you weak and hold you back in life. All of my examples were based on real life, not on scholarly or scientific articles. I just explained what the sins are and what they look like in everyday life.

Now, we've arrived at the other side, and it's time to look at positive qualities, good deeds, and kind intentions. Here again, I'm not going to be summarising for you what scholars have said on the topic. Instead, I'll give you simple, clear examples so you can find the virtues in your own life.

People always think it's the animal instincts, or sins, that motivate people to earn money and do well in life. I'm here to tell you that people who succeed that way are full of greed and fear. There's a better way to succeed. Instead of letting greed and anger and pride drive you, you can rely on your virtues to live a life that is full of both success and joy. A life where you get to express your truest self.

Pay close attention to your heart when you read this section. As I describe each of the virtues, that virtue will wake up inside of you, and you'll see how different your life could be if you worked on strengthening that virtue. You'll start to react differently to situations and make different decisions. This is the most serious part of the book, and I don't want you to miss it.

But before we get started analysing the virtues, I want you to grab your phone or a pencil and make a list of all the positive qualities you see in people. Don't worry about guessing all seven of the virtues. This isn't a graded assignment! And don't use Google. I'm not trying to test your research skills. Instead, I want you to spend some time thinking about the good traits you've noticed in the people around you and write them down.

I'll wait right here until you get back.

Now that you're in the right frame of mind, let's look at the seven virtues that are the opposites of the seven deadly sins. You're going to learn a lot here. What makes these virtues so good for you? How can they help you? How are they interconnected? You'll find the answers to practical questions like these and much more.

Prudence

What do you think when you hear the word prudence? Write down your own personal definition—without looking it up. Then keep reading so I can guide you to how I understand the name of this virtue.

I never went to seminary. I didn't even finish college. So, I'm going to keep the explanation and the definition simple. Think back to the sins we learned about in the first part of the book. The first sin was pride. We learned that pride involves being an egotist and thinking of yourself first. Prudence is the opposite of pride. A prudent person thinks without egotism; they think like a creator, not a destroyer. When you're prudent, your intention is to create good things for yourself and others. That's the opposite of egotism. A prudent person cares about their community and the rest of the world. Put very simply, I would define prudence as thinking about yourself and others positively and with kindness.

Why is prudence a positive trait? Because it allows you to live and create in the world without hurting the people around you. It's a more honest way to live. You follow your conscience without creating problems for your community. In your relationships, you're focused on growth, not on competition. You want everyone to live well and experience kindness. Prudence is when you don't call your friend early in the morning because you don't want to wake them up. If you were an egotist, you wouldn't care that they're asleep.

Here's another example of prudent thinking: your neighbour is an expert at something—maybe they're a good gardener or financial planner—and you want to ask them for advice. Because you're prudent, though, you understand that your neighbour's time is valuable. And when they take the time to help you out, you don't just say "thanks!" and run off. You make sure to reciprocate. You think about your neighbour's point of view and their interests. That's prudence.

Prudence affects your relationships with other people, but it also plays an important role in how you value your own time and money. An imprudent person spends all their money on new clothes or online poker and is surprised when they can't make rent the next month. An imprudent person stays out late drinking and misses work the following day. Or rides a motorcycle without a helmet. Prudence makes you consider the future and behave in ways that will benefit you and those around you. Imprudence just makes you a danger to yourself and others.

Imprudence is fuelled by egotism. If you gamble away all your money at a casino, it's because egotism paints illusions that you're going to win big. And you believe it. You believe that product of your mind.

In the examples above, do you see where prudence is fuelled by kindness? You take the time to consider everyone's interests and the possible outcomes of your actions because you want your community to flourish. And since everything is interconnected, that same prudence helps you succeed, too.

Question and Answers about Prudence

Question: I want to ask a friend to help me with a project that will eventually benefit them, too. The benefits to me will be a little greater than the benefits to them. Should I offer something additional in exchange? I want my friend to know that I care about their interests.

That's a very good question. You're on the right track. Whenever I have dealings with a person, I try to make sure that they come out a little bit ahead of me. I know that God is judging me on how I treat people, and I don't want to gain a few percentage points and lose my soul. That's a good, prudent way to live. But you see, prudence isn't a set of rules you can memorise. It isn't a step-by-step guide to doing business ethically. There are plenty of sinful people who try to game the system. They think, 'If I get this certification or join that non-profit, people will think I'm running an ethical business.' But prudence is something that happens inside your soul.

Before you get discouraged, I want you to know that, for now, it's enough that you're reading my book and thinking about what prudence should look like in your life. That alone will wake up the prudence that is already present in your soul.

Question: Are you talking about prudence first because it's the most important virtue? Or is it the first virtue that all the other virtues build off of?

Here's another interesting question. I don't have a ready answer to it, though, because if the virtues are a ladder, I'm climbing it with you. When we get to the end, I'll have a more complete answer. If you look back at the first section on sins, the first sin we discussed was pride. And it turned out that pride was tangled up in all the other sins, too. I won't be surprised at all if the same is true with the virtues.

Question: Would it be correct to say that prudence is a way we can express love for ourselves and others?

Exactly. When you're prudent, you avoid harming yourself and other people. Why? Because you love yourself and your friends and family. You love your colleagues and partners. And that love causes you to be prudent in your actions.

Question: You said that prudence is an honest way of living. Do you mean being honest with others?

Exactly. In all your dealings with people, never forget to consider their interests. You can't ignore other people's interests and still be prudent. When I work with a person, I always ask them right off the bat what they need from our collaboration in order to be happy. Or if I already know what they want, I go ahead and offer it. I like to say that I don't have any unpaid debts. Even if the person I'm dealing with offers to help me out for free, I repay the debt. This goes for financial or work-related issues and favours between friends.

Question: Is it possible to take prudence to the extreme?

That wouldn't be prudence anymore, would it? Imagine a person who doesn't really care about others but wants to play by the rules and get along so they can be successful. So, they think, "I'll help all my co-workers, whether they ask me to or not. Then they'll all owe me favours." If you've been on the receiving end of this kind of help, you know it feels wrong and unnatural. Prudence is never extreme.

Question: Can a person have the virtue of prudence and the sin of pride at the same time?

No, never at the same time. You might be a prudent person who fell prey to temptation. If one person saw you behaving prudently and another person saw you acting on pride, then they might wonder if you had both the sin and the virtue at the same time. In reality, you changed. We are always changing and growing. But a person can't maintain a prudent life while also being driven by pride. That part of your soul can either be light or dark; it can't be both simultaneously. When you get rid of the pride in your soul, that same space fills up with prudence, and you start acting with care and kindness.

Question: The way you explain it, a prudent person always knows what they owe the people around them. If you're surrounded by sinful, evil people, won't they just abuse your kindness?

That can happen at a certain stage in your development. People have abused my kindness in the past. I watched it happen. But I never get angry at people when they try to use me, because pointing your finger and blaming others is always the wrong answer. Even when you know they are, in fact, behaving badly. The only person you can point the finger at is yourself. If someone takes advantage of you or uses you, then it's your fault for not recognising that behaviour in time. You choose who gets to be in your life, so you're the one who needs to work on yourself.

I always say that each of us is always growing, and that's true here, too. Just because you made a mistake and let a person take advantage of you doesn't mean you're a bad or hopeless person. I've been through it myself. I used to think,

"Maybe they'll change," but in the end I always realised that people show you who they are. If they don't abuse your trust, they'll do it to someone else. That's just how they treat people. Most of them do it without even thinking about it. They're zombies.

Once you have some experience, you realise that you shouldn't let people like that get close to you. They're the wrong people for you. Instead, make friends and do business with people who are kind and reliable. You treat them fairly, and they do the same to you. That one change will drastically improve your quality of life.

That's my position on being kind and considerate in a world full of egotists. You wouldn't tell a cactus to stop being spiny, would you? It's the same here. Don't lecture the cactus. Just stop touching it.

Question: You make it sound like the opposite of egotism is victimhood.

Yes and no. When I've covered this topic in my video lectures, it always creates a lot of discussion. If you think about it, the Christian saints were always martyrs because they were living according to their faith and practicing the virtues, but the people around them threw stones at them. The hard part is that you can't throw stones back when you're living virtuously. That's the whole point. It's hard, but that's how it works.

And you know what? The practice of virtue makes you stronger. When people throw stones at me, the most I can do is answer back with words. I can't retaliate in any form. But here's the cool thing: there are lots of people in this big world, and living virtuously attracts the people who value you. The negative people won't go anywhere, but your life starts to revolve more around the good people you find.

You should never answer back when someone tries to provoke you or speaks harshly about you. Even if you have all the time in the world. Because retribution does nothing but strengthen your mind and your sins. Instead, try to avoid conflict. If your upstairs neighbour is having a loud party late at night, don't bother getting worked up about it. Don't give in to feelings of resentment and aggression. Just accept the world the way it is and move on with your life. The only person you have a right to criticise is yourself. Instead of complaining about the neighbour, work hard to improve your quality of life. Make it a goal to move somewhere with better neighbours. A sinful person will call the police on the neighbour, but that's weakness. That's cowardice.

If I buy a t-shirt from an online store and it turns out that the seller is a scammer who mails out random junk instead of the items people order, I'm not going to waste my time trying to track them down and punish them. It's my fault that I didn't check the seller's reviews first. See how it works? When some people get scammed, they waste their time and mental energy trying to fight back. I've seen people waste so much time on the phone or in court that their hair falls out. A lot of the people I consult with end up in situations like this, and they ask me, "What else can I do to make this right?" I always answer, "Just let it go. You have more to lose than the person who did you wrong." I tell them they shouldn't have sent money to a scammer or whatever it was they did that started the whole ball rolling. When you get embroiled in a conflict with someone, your mind spins at top speed and your heart shuts down. That's exactly what the devils want. It's all a trap.

I've been posting verses from the Bible to my Telegram account, and all the verses point to the same idea of turning the other cheek, which is something I've been writing about since I was in high school. The things I've been thinking about my whole life were spelled out for us in the Bible thousands of years ago. This is the foundation of success: not how sharp your sword is or how big your gun is, but how virtuously you live.

"Having people's respect is not good. Such a person will do wrong for a piece of bread." That verse comes from Proverbs, and it means that you shouldn't be artificial just to get ahead. Here's another one: "Whoever rebukes a person will in the end gain favour, rather than one who has a flattering tongue." When I tell people the truth, they see that as me rebuking them, and they don't like it. But it's better for them than if I told them what they wanted to hear.

I'm always surprised to look back and see how closely I've been following the Bible since childhood. A lot of people hated me for it, but I knew I was doing the right thing.

Here's another verse: "Those who lead good people along an evil path will fall into their own trap, but the honest will inherit good things." There are so many people out there looking to trap you with materialism or drugs or even worse.

"He that turns away his ear from hearing the law, even his prayer shall be abomination." Sinful people don't understand my books. They think I'm running a sect. But I'd rather let them throw their stones than react in anger. That's how I choose to live my life.

"Better the poor whose walk is blameless than the rich whose ways are perverse." That means it's better to be poor and kind than rich and sinful. That was one of the first choices I made as a young man. I left college and left home to avoid temptations because I wanted to live with integrity. I realised I'd rather be a starving writer than succeed according to the world's rules. Back then, I had no idea what my choice would lead me to. I just knew I didn't want to work at a job where I had to flatter and fool people. The criticism was fierce. People said, "Why should anyone read your books if you aren't already rich and successful?" But here's the thing: nobody says that to me anymore.

"The wicked flee when no one pursues them, but the righteous are bold as a lion." What does that mean? A sinful person is always on the run. They're always afraid of being late, they're always living in the future, always running after something. They think someone is always trying to catch up with them. Sin is a stressful way to live. When in fact, the truth is always right there in front of you. You don't have to chase after it. Imagine this: you can change your whole life—physically, financially—without moving a muscle, just by turning on the light in your soul. That one change costs nothing, but once you embrace it, your whole life will be transformed. That's the true secret.

Do you remember the book *The Secret*? It came out over a decade ago and promoted the idea of positive thinking or manifesting or whatever you want to call it. The book basically told you that if you want a Lamborghini or a mega yacht, you have to hang a photo of the object you desire on your fridge and look at it every day. Somehow, the power of your thoughts is supposed to attract that object into your life. The secret I'm talking about is nothing like that. The Bible has plenty to say about chasing after wealth. If you make kindness to yourself and others the foundation of your life, then your material problems will take care of themselves. If you need something, you'll have it. That is not the same as saying, "Dream it and you'll get it." The people who focus on their wants instead of on the virtues are walking down a dead-end road.

Question: Do I have to repay a favour if I find out the person did the favour so they could hold it over me?

I feel like you're stretching really hard to find an exception to the rule that a prudent person should repay favours and consider the interests of their partners and friends. If I hire a person to do some work for me and what they do isn't up to par, then I pay them anyway because I don't want to create a conflict. I'll remember the screw up, but I'll pay. If someone doesn't live up to their side of a bargain with me, I fulfil my own obligations and tell them, "God bless you." My heart is clean. But I know that something awful will happen to the person who tried to cheat me. That's one of the laws of nature. So, it doesn't matter if you suspect or even know for a fact that someone helped you out because they want to ask you for something later. Let them have it. The most important thing is that you are not the one to cause conflict.

Question: Are there any actions I can take to become more prudent?

Definitely. Just as the seven sins are strengthened by actions, you can do things to build up your virtues. When someone comes to visit you, give them the best bed in the house, even if you usually sleep there. Let your friend or significant other choose what movie you watch. Every time you behave unselfishly, you get bonus points from above. It's true. And if you're selfish and egotistical, life will punish you. The people I know who ignore this truth are still poor, depressed, and driven by sin.

The only way to reinforce any of the virtues is through good deeds. But you have to do your good deeds sincerely, from the heart. Don't expect people to praise you for them. The minute you do something nice for someone with the expectation that they will like you better or want to do business with you, you're being driven by sin instead of by virtue. That's the norm in society, isn't it? We expect that if we do someone a good turn, they'll do us a good turn later. But if you're prudent, you do the good deed without expecting something in return. If the person you lent a hand to never responds in kind, that's on them. Your goal isn't fairness. Your goal isn't to get as much as you give. All those accounts are kept in Heaven, not on Earth.

Question: You talked about how people are born with different souls and different levels of experience. Are there people who will never attain prudence in their lifetime?

I want you to think a little deeper about what it means to be born into the world with a soul, with experience. If there is sin in you when you're born, that doesn't mean you're condemned to live with it all your life. That's just the level you're at on day one. You have a whole lifetime to grow and change.

From the day we're born, our job is to let go of the illusions that the world hands us—relationships, work, hobbies—and learn to know our own souls and strengthen our virtues. That's the purpose of our lives here on Earth: to grow.

Question: Are there any bad deeds that take away a person's prudence right away?

Any time you are underhanded or act for your own gain, you risk losing your prudence. Here are some examples: you have a party and invite the people you want to be seen with instead of the people you love; or you invite someone to go on a weekend trip with you because you want someone to pay half the costs; or you have a cigarette outside with your boss at lunch so you can find out about opportunities before other people hear about them.

Sneaky behaviour like that is always punished in the end. This is one of the biggest things I warn people about. People think they're being smart, when in fact they're being deceitful and dishonest.

It can be a fine line, though. Let's talk through it so you can see the difference between being devious and just being confident. Imagine you're trying out for a part in a movie. The line goes around the block. It looks like you might not even get into the building. So, you go up to the security guards and tell them you were personally invited by the director. That's a lie, and it's a dishonest attempt to get ahead. But what if you're just standing in line and the director walks by? There's nothing wrong with stopping them and saying, "Hey, I'm looking forward to trying out. Is there any chance you could listen to me right now?" That's just being confident and taking a risk (as long as you respond gracefully if the director refuses). Honesty is what makes the difference.

Question: Why do you define prudence as thinking with kindness about people? I thought that we were supposed to stop thinking and listen to our hearts.

Let's look at this closer. I don't want you to walk away with questions in your mind. The information I lay out in this book is supposed to be as simple as possible so you can act on it without having to do any mental gymnastics on your own.

When I say your mind is the problem, I mean the instincts and reactions that control you instead of you controlling them. Buddhists call that the restless mind or monkey mind. They teach that you can calm it down, but you can't get rid of your monkey mind—it's always going to be there. But there's another aspect to your mind, the part that you use to think and analyse. When you calm what the Buddhists call your restless or monkey mind, the rest of your mind is able to think and analyse information without being interrupted. That's what I mean when I say you need to turn off your mind and live by your heart. I don't mean that I want the space between your ears to be empty.

Question: What about extreme sports? If I go bungee jumping, do I forfeit my prudence because I'm doing something dangerous?

That's a great question! I hope my answer will explain once and for all why I don't do any extreme sports. Let me start by saying that I'm not afraid of dying. So, why don't I jump out of airplanes or off bridges? Because there is always an element of arrogance in taking those kinds of risks for fun, and the Bible is very clear on God's attitude toward people who are arrogant. Do not tempt God. That's a message you see throughout the Bible.

If you don't have a practical reason for going bungee jumping—and what practical reason could there be?—then it isn't prudent. Prudence means considering your actions and making sure that everything you do benefits your community and your soul. Jumping off a bridge for fun doesn't make the cut.

There are plenty of actions that could go either way in terms of their prudence. If you buy a car to get to work or school, you're being prudent. If, on the other hand, you buy a car so you can drag race in parking lots at night, then you're headed for trouble. It's all about the intent.

Question: If I understand correctly, you're asking us to quiet our minds and let our souls take control. In psychology and esoterica, we call that 'enlightenment.' Is that what you mean?

Exactly. When you're driven by sin, you're unenlightened. You act based on your instincts. When you let your soul be in charge, you reach a higher level. You become enlightened.

But I'm hearing another question underneath the one you asked. If you're wondering whether you can achieve the same level of enlightenment through psychotherapy, then my answer is a definite 'no.' Because most of the therapists you'll encounter aren't going to help you tune in to your soul.

Imagine a woman who struggles with anxiety. She signs up with a therapist in hopes of finding relief, and the therapist tells her to read upon feminism and learn how to climb over people so she can get what she wants. Is that going to help her find enlightenment? Of course not. It won't even help her deal with her anxiety.

People assume that I intersect somehow with the world of psychology and mental health, but nothing could be farther from the truth. I'm just a regular person telling it like it is. What tools do the brain doctors have? Drugs, and not much else. My tools are prayer and meditation and hard work. Going on a pilgrimage is better for you than getting a diagnosis and going on antidepressants.

Question: You've said several times that people shouldn't actively seek pleasure. Does that mean that you can't be prudent and also be trying to achieve joy or satisfaction?

When you are working on strengthening your virtues and weakening your sin—even if you haven't finished the journey yet—your focus is on building and doing. You don't have time to sit back and daydream and let yourself be pleasured by illusions. Those illusions are just created by your mind. Things like passive income, a beach vacation, or parties every weekend are just fantasies. They're like a drug that affects your mind.

Everything in your life should have a purpose. If I go to Brazil, it's because I set up meetings with some local businessmen there. I have an idea for a business, maybe importing steaks or opening a restaurant. Something practical.

Sure, I can spend an afternoon at the beach or sit in cafes in the evenings. But the whole reason for the trip is practical. So many people fail to grasp that life is supposed to have a purpose. They go to Bora Bora or Costa Rica or the Azores because their friends all went. Ask them what they're going to do there, and they don't even know. "Just sit on the beach, I guess." That's the best they can come up with. It's cold where they live in London or Chicago, and they want to go somewhere warm.

I believe that chasing after pleasure this way is the opposite of prudent. And it's just plain wrong. Warming your backsides on the beach can't be the goal of your life. Understand this: I'm not trying to offend anyone, but I'm also not worried about making everyone like me, because my life is built on faith. I'd rather tell the truth than be popular. I'd rather have five followers who love and are healed by my message than twenty million followers who are there for the beach photos (which I'm not posting, anyway).

Question: Can you describe the prudent way to fast?

Some people fast, others don't. And don't think that fasting makes you cleaner or more virtuous, because plenty of sinful people give up meat for Lent. They do it to look holy or because they're afraid not to. There are all sorts of bad reasons to observe a fast. And there are plenty of good, virtuous people who don't fast, usually because they don't have enough willpower yet, but sometimes for other reasons. So, you can't compare people based on their ability to fast. Try not to be so literal-minded about faith. There's more to virtue than following the rules.

Question: Is it ever okay to sin in order to accomplish a prudent goal?

That's one heck of a question. I've always said that the human mind is diabolically clever, and that question takes the cake.

A truly virtuous person wouldn't think this way. They would listen to their conscience. If you're tying yourself in knots looking for a justification for something you know is wrong but you want to do it anyway, then you'd better take a hard look at the sin in your heart. There are no two ways about it.

Question: My father taught me to put other people first, but in his own life, he always gets really upset if someone doesn't treat him the same way. How can I unlearn those childhood lessons?

Posing that question shows that you're on the right path. I don't see a contradiction in your father's behaviour. He was at a level of spiritual development where he was able to do the right thing, but he was upset when others didn't follow his example. When you grow and reach a higher level, you can behave with prudence and consider the interests of the people around you without expecting them to do the same for you. To get there, you have to cultivate all seven of the virtues we're going to be looking at.

Every person is a mixture of sins and virtues. You might have four really strong virtues and three sins that all turn on and off depending on the circumstances you find yourself in. It's a fine line for most people. Listen to the wrong album, hang out with the wrong people, and your dark side is in the driver's seat. But the opposite is also true: you can grow in wonderful ways and become stronger than the people who raised you. The journey is all about hope.

Question: Can a person be virtuous if they do all the right things because they were raised that way, even if they don't understand the underlying values and would never use the words 'sin' or 'virtue?'

That's another good question. It shows you're thinking.

When you do good deeds, they have to come from the heart, not just because you have a set of rules you obey. You have to be actively following your conscience. Those are the actions that will help you grow and earn you points from above.

Working out because you feel bad about your body or because you want to impress people is not at all the same as working out because you care about your health or because you're trying to complete a fitness challenge. The actions look the same from the outside, but as I'm always reminding you, it's what inside that counts.

If your parents taught you the right way to behave but you follow those rules like a robot or because you're still afraid of getting in trouble, then you're still being driven by your mind and by sin.

The line between good behaviour and bad behaviour is confusing until you look at the intent. That's what this whole book is about: looking at your true intentions.

Question: There are two things in my life that really bother me. First, I was in a car accident and I know the other driver set me up. My insurance paid their claim, so now I'm paying higher premiums and I can't let it go. I'm really upset about what happened. Second, I've been moving a lot because no matter where I rent, I end up with bad neighbours. You say to ignore people and stop reacting to them, but I'm not at that level yet. What can I do to stop being so upset about both situations?

You understand my message, and I want to commend you for that. You've already attained a certain level of virtue. You're working on your sins. You know you have to stop blaming other people for everything. But really annoying things—sometimes even scary things—keep happening and you feel like your virtues aren't strong enough to help you stay on an even keel. So, you're frustrated.

If you want to stop being angry at your neighbours or at the random cheaters who cross your path, literally and figuratively, you have to become even more spiritual than you are now. You've made progress, but you have to keep working. Say, you're driven 10% by virtue and 90% by sin. That 10% makes you prudent enough to see that you have to stop arguing with the neighbours and moving all the time, and it tells you not to let that one dishonest driver spoil the rest of your life. But your temper still boils over when you think about it. Your animal instincts are in charge. If you don't want that to happen, you have to grow your virtues through meditation, prayer, and good deeds.

It isn't enough to merely stamp out your sins. The fact that you get upset at your neighbours all the time shows that you need to actively cultivate the virtues that are missing in your life. Once your heart is full of love, you'll feel stronger in those situations that used to upset you. That's the whole point of this book.

Question: Is it prudent to give handouts to the homeless?

That's a painfully difficult question to answer. As always, it depends on your own thoughts and intentions. Before we get into those intentions, I want to warn you against responding in fear or anger when people ask you for handouts. We live in an imperfect world, full of broken people whose needs—financial or emotional—are greater than what they or their loved ones can meet. Don't be afraid of people who ask you for help. And don't go to the opposite extreme of getting angry. This is the world we live in, and we should always react with love, not fear or anger.

When you give a handout to someone on the street, make sure you aren't trying to check off a box. 'Charity: done.' It has to be spontaneous, and it has to come from the heart. You're walking down the street and see an older man propped up against a wall with his legs in a sleeping bag. You happen to have some cash in your pocket, so you reach out and give it to him. Seeing a need and meeting that need—without making a big deal out of it—is always virtuous.

At the same time, I don't want to encourage you to give money to people who are actively begging, either asking for money or holding a little cardboard sign. Most of the people who are out there begging are driven by sin. No, not all of them, but most. No matter how sad their stories are, they're getting what they deserve. Since you would have to be a mind reader to see the difference, just don't give money to beggars. Don't feed their sin.

Please don't think I'm saying you should never help anyone. If your friend has a job interview and you offer to watch their kid, that's great. If you need help moving your stuff to a new apartment and your friends come over to lend a hand, that's beautiful. That's how people are supposed to help each other. But giving money to beggars doesn't really help them. It just keeps them on the street longer. And giving money to an alcoholic relative does the same thing: it just lets them stay addicted. When you see someone who is being punished by life, don't get involved. You don't want to be on that frequency. I've seen so many of my readers suffer because they keep trying to help a relative who has addiction issues. Why is that so wrong? Because it isn't your job. You're trying to take on a burden that isn't yours to carry.

Question: If I ride a motorcycle without a helmet, then I'm guilty of being imprudent. But if I wear a helmet, doesn't that mean I'm afraid of getting hurt? I thought that faith in God meant letting go of fear.

Remember: don't tempt God. A prudent person wears a helmet not because they're afraid or because they doubt God; they wear it because they know that

God helps those who help themselves. If you think you can race around on a motorcycle with no helmet and God's going to protect you, you have another thing coming. Your family is going to hate to see you drinking from a straw in your hospital bed. That's how harsh the punishment for imprudence can be.

A prudent person wears a helmet because they understand the risks. They trust in God, but they also respect the reality of the world we live in, with double-parked delivery trucks and open manholes.

Question: I'm a terrible procrastinator. Does that mean I need to work on developing prudence?

I can't answer your question without more information. What kinds of things do you procrastinate on, and why? If a prudent person puts off making a decision or taking an action, they know why they're waiting. But a person who is driven by instinct and lives in a dreamland of illusions puts things off so they can keep dreaming. Do you see the difference? So, it all depends on why you procrastinate. Your reasons might very well be prudent, but then again they might not.

Let's say, your father comes to visit you, and you postpone a work project so you can spend time with him. Both of you are usually busy, and you haven't hung out with him in person for years. That's good and prudent.

But if you postpone projects all the time for reasons you don't even understand, just because you feel like it, then that's a sign of chaos in your life. That's imprudent.

Question: If I understand you correctly, a prudent person is also a person who follows their heart. Does that mean that if I'm prudent, then I can follow through with any idea I have and know that God approves?

You're starting to understand. A lot of my readers write in and ask me if they can take this or that job or sell certain kinds of things. I always reply that if they're meeting a need, if someone needs the job they do or the thing they sell, then they're doing fine.

This topic came up again right at the start of the pandemic. I was giving a lecture on personal growth, and the topic of how different jobs contribute to society came up. People were seeing doctors and nurses struggling, and that made them think about how their own jobs affect their lives and their communities. I told them that the jobs that serve a purpose are the ones that help people, and that you can tell how virtuous a person is by the job they have. Imagine a person who says that their job is important because they develop pharmaceuticals. On the face of it, that sounds like an essential job, something that a prudent person would do to care for their community. But what if that same person is actually looking to profit off the community's fear? They aren't concerned with public health and safety. They just want to rake in the profits while everyone is afraid. As always, what matters is the intention behind the action.

Question: I have another noisy neighbour question. I don't want problems with my neighbours, but I need to find a friendly, kind way of explaining to them that their noise bothers us. Is that possible?

Before we talk about your possible reactions, let's look at what kind of people your neighbours are. We can already say that they are egotistical and driven by sin because they don't care about the effect they're having on the people around them. If you approach them calmly, they're either going to pretend to be shocked and give you a half-hearted apology, or they're going to blow up at you. I don't want you to get punched in the face.

I'm no psychiatrist. This is basic logic. It's like a mathematical model that works the same way every time. When you have a neighbour being loud late at night, you already know they don't care about you.

When I was younger, I had friends who played loud music all night. I'd say, "Hey, turn it down! People are trying to sleep," and they would just laugh, like they thought all those other people didn't exist. That's how sick some people are.

But how are we supposed to react to that? Here's my answer: we aren't supposed to react at all. That's the prudent response to someone who isn't in their right mind. After all, it isn't our job to educate them about how they affect the people around them. Life will do that soon enough. Maybe they'll get sick, or they'll be arrested, or they'll get in a car accident. But until life teaches them those hard lessons, they won't believe that the people around them exist. They won't believe anything you tell them.

Remember what I told you at the beginning of this book? Don't provoke others, and don't let them provoke you. You don't have anything to gain by letting noisy neighbours distract you from your own life. Here's how I think of it: my life is great. I'm writing books and giving lectures. I'm learning more and more about life and how we're supposed to live it. I'm always in motion. So, there's no way I'm going to stop and go argue with my neighbour about his music. If someone hits my car, I'll let my insurance to handle the paperwork. I won't lose even a minute of sleep over it. There was a time when I would have gotten upset about those kinds of situations, but now I've learned better and I do better.

Fortitude

Like the other virtues, fortitude—call it bravery or courage if you want—is a product of awareness. While the sins are animal instincts, the virtues are those qualities that come from meditation and consideration.

When we think of examples of bravery, we tend to put it in a fairy-tale context: think of the knight saving the fair lady, or the peasant standing up to the lord of the manor. But we can find plenty of instances of fortitude closer to home in the twenty-first century. Here's one: if you've ever told your boss the unvarnished truth when you knew they wouldn't be happy about it, that's fortitude. If you've ever reached out a hand to someone who was hurting, that's fortitude. Willpower and courage like that strengthen your faith.

I can hear you thinking, "You said that it was a waste of time to try to help people, and now you're saying that we're brave if we reach out to someone who's in trouble. Which is it?" Well, it depends on the situation and on your motivations. You're the only one who knows for sure if you're acting out of courage and fortitude or out of sin.

When I was a young kid, I had a friend who lived way out in the country. His family got their water from a well. A bunch of us were out there playing one day, and one of the boys started fooling around and fell in the well. He caught onto a bar part of the way down, so he didn't fall all the way to the bottom. I could see him in there. The other kids all ran off because they were afraid of getting in trouble with the adults. But I wasn't afraid. I climbed in as far as I could and pulled him out, even though he was bigger and heavier than me. I was just a kid, but my faith was already strong. And faith is the opposite of fear. None of the virtues—especially fortitude—are accessible without faith.

There are people who jump in to help because they're trying to show off or prove to the world and to themselves that they're strong and brave. Don't let them fool you. True bravery is when it's a serious situation and you become an instrument of God to save someone's life.

But fortitude is about more than saving people. It's also about recognising and accepting them. It's about being open and accepting yourself. Fear finds so many places to hide in our lives. It often looks like shame. Fortitude is the opposite of that fear.

When you're afraid, you make excuses. Once you have fortitude, though, the excuses stop. You admit it when you're wrong and get back to work. If you break something, you tell the owner. If you don't know what to do on a work project, you're upfront about it with your co-workers. If you're at fault in a car accident, you stick around and make it right. If you promised to attend an event but something comes up, you tell the truth instead of making up an excuse. That's the way to live. Accepting reality is brave. Don't wait for reality to catch up with you. Accept it right away.

Fortitude is such a rare virtue these days that I can count the truly brave people in my life on the fingers of one hand. Everyone loves to watch movies about courageous heroes, but where are the heroes in real life? When I was younger, I used to think I'd been born in the wrong century. Now, I understand that we can't wait for heroes. We have to grow up to *be* them.

Questions and Answers about Fortitude

Over the years, I've noticed that some of my readers associate bravery with men for some reason. That's a shallow understanding of the concept. We aren't talking about physical domination. We're talking about courage and hope, which are qualities any human can possess.

Question: I am a rock climber, and I've learned that courage doesn't mean being fearless; it means conquering your fear. When I first started climbing, I wasn't afraid of anything because I hadn't been in any scary situations yet. After a bad fall, however, I realised I was afraid to climb again. I had to work on being brave now that I knew what could happen. Would you agree that fortitude is about mastering fear?

Exactly! Fortitude means getting past your fear. People who say they aren't afraid of anything are either lying to themselves or they're too stupid to realise all the things that could go wrong. When children do dangerous things, it's not because they're aware of the risks and demonstrating their faith and courage. They simply don't have the better judgment that comes with life experience.

In the section on prudence, someone asked me about extreme sports like bungee jumping, and I shared my view that taking unnecessary risks is imprudent. I want to add here that jumping off a bridge for fun isn't courageous, either. Courage is when you have to do something hard or dangerous, and you know the risks involved, but you do it anyway because you know it's the right thing to do.

Question: When you were talking about prudence, you said that trying to help people never works. Now you're saying that it's courageous to reach out and offer help. Which is true?

You have to have reached a high level of awareness or enlightenment before you can help people who have serious problems in their lives. Otherwise, nothing you do will work. You'll try to help people for all the wrong reasons—so you can feel better about yourself, or because you feel guilty, or because you want to show off how perfect your life is—and you'll only end up hurting your friends and relatives and getting hurt yourself.

Working side-by-side with people to reach a goal is different. Instead of riding in like a knight on a white horse, you get into the trenches with people and work hard to make something happen that will benefit everyone. That's an entirely different kind of help. Sometimes, both kinds of help take courage, but don't confuse the two.

Question: How can I tell if my courage is coming from my heart or from my head?

It always depends on how you feel. If your reaction to an emergency is to start overthinking it, then you're being driven by your mind. If you feel clear in your head and warm in your chest, then your heart is in control. That's how you can test yourself. Check in with your feelings before you act.

Question: Now that I'm reading your book, I'm starting to remember times in the past when I did the wrong thing and hurt people, and it's making me sad. How should I feel about mistakes I made a long time ago?

It's hard to give a single answer to this question that covers every possible situation from your past. But I know you should never beat yourself up when you look back at mistakes. What's the point of learning to do better if you're just going to stay stuck worrying about what you did wrong before? A person with strong virtues will look back on their own mistakes with understanding, just like they look at other people's mistakes with understanding. They would understand that they've grown since then.

So, my advice is to look forward instead of looking back. Don't obsess about the past. Instead, work on strengthening your virtues so that, ten years from now, you'll be proud to look back at yourself the way you are today. Do good deeds. Surround yourself with kind people and positive messages. Allow yourself to feel positive about your future.

To those of you who are reading along and thinking that the virtues sound awesome and you can't wait to get started leveraging their power, I want to say this: don't get ahead of yourself. Keep reading. Make sure you understand. To those of you who are following along and starting to feel bad about how you behaved in the past when you didn't have all this information about sin and virtue, my message is different: keep your chin up. The fact that you're reacting so strongly to my book shows that you understand the core of my message and you're ready to benefit from it. This is exactly the right time for you to make some changes.

Question: Many years ago, I stole something from my employer. From the point of view of fortitude, should I go back and tell them now?

I don't think you should go digging up the past. What happened, happened. Life has probably already punished you for what you did, so start living right and don't look back.

In previous books, I've referred to deep, serious problems from your past as knots that you have to untie before you can continue to grow. What I had in mind was things like broken relationships. Say, you hurt a friend or family member badly and never apologised. Once you realise the harm you caused, you have to go back and admit your fault so you can move on and grow as a person. But there's no need to go hunting for someone from your past who might not even remember you just so you can tell them your sad story and apologise. That would be overdoing it.

Justice

I want to make one thing clear from the start: justice as a human virtue is not the same thing as social justice. Justice is something you have to *do*, while social justice is something you demand from other people. Ironically, I see a lot of people driven by sin in their fight for social justice. They're so focused on the evils of other people that they neglect to examine their own hearts. In this book, we're only interested in justice on a personal level, because that's the only level you can control.

So, what is justice? Let's work our way to a definition. Like prudence, justice has a lot to do with the ability to put your thoughts and actions in the context of your wider community. Looking at its opposite can be helpful: people who are unjust are also greedy and egotistical. They want more than what you have. They treat their relationships as resources to be exploited. When you believe in justice, you aren't driven by your ego. You understand that you're surrounded by your family, friends, neighbours, co-workers, and the rest of the people in your community. While you keep your own interests in mind, you're fair and also consider their interests.

Justice means being fair. Taking credit for something you did with help from a co-worker is unfair. If you want to be just, you have to explain how your co-worker contributed to the success of the project.

Here's another example: I'm looking through some nature photos I took and my friend convinced me to try to sell some of them. If they end up selling, then justice tells me that I ought to give my friend half of the money I made. After all, if they hadn't encouraged me, I might have deleted the photos or filed them away and forgotten about them.

Justice means telling the truth. If your neighbour borrows tools from you and forgets to give them back, the next time they ask you if they can borrow something you may be tempted to make up a lie. "I don't have an extension cord." Or "My drill isn't working." But when you live according to justice, you have to tell the truth. You have to say, "I've loaned you tools before and you didn't return them, so I'd rather not loan you anything else." No apologies, just the truth.

Being fair doesn't always mean sympathising with people when they make mistakes. If your roommate complains that their wallet was stolen at a nightclub, a fair person sees that they are the cause of their own trouble. Instead of doing homework or going to bed early, your roommate went out looking for adventure in a place where people go to revel in sin. So, it's no surprise that they came home without their wallet. It could have been worse. When you understand justice, you know that good behaviour is rewarded, while imprudent behaviour is punished.

That doesn't mean that we get to judge other people's behaviour. We can see it and draw our own conclusions without judging. The only judge is God. If someone hurts you and you want to hurt them back to make things 'fair,' think again. That's revenge. That's sin.

So many people think that justice is all about fighting injustice. Aggressive, greedy, or despairing people hear 'justice' and start to get angry. They think it's all about forcing other people to stop whatever it is they're doing that isn't just. But that's all wrong. There's no such thing as 'demanding justice.' When you demand that someone else be fair, you're allowing your sin to drive you. Instead, I want you to think about practicing *your own* kindness and being fair with people.

All of the virtues are interconnected. As soon as you work on prudence, you'll find yourself being fairer with people, and vice versa. And as I keep telling you, this process—turning on our virtues and turning off our sins—is the whole reason humans are alive on Earth. Everything else is just an illusion.

When I look up how writers and philosophers have talked about justice throughout history, this is what I find: Thomas Aquinas said that justice is the opposite of greed. In the New Testament, Matthew says much the same thing: "Blessed are they who hunger after righteousness." In other words, we are supposed to hunger for justice, not for material things. In ancient Rome, the Goddess Justicia held a scale to show consideration for more than one point of view. Some commentators talked about how justice meant getting what you deserve. All of those definitions point to the same thing: justice means not putting yourself first, not putting your finger on the scale.

Do you remember the definition of greed? A greedy person puts themselves first and wants everything for themselves. So, a fair, just person considers those around them. They don't forget about their people. That right there is justice.

In short, you want to follow the path of justice to avoid sin and punishment.

Questions and Answers about Justice

Question: I always feel like I owe everyone. Is that my sense of justice, or is it something else?

I've worked with lots of unhappy people who feel inferior or feel like they owe the world something all the time. But that's a mistake. Think of a young adult child who pays off their parent's debts because they feel like they owe that parent for raising them. Think of the person who loans a friend money all the time and never gets paid back. Think of the parent who always steps up and saves their child from the consequences of their mistakes. In all those situations, the person might be attempting to help out of fear or feelings of inferiority, but they aren't acting out of a sense of justice.

Whenever you feel like you have to do something for another person or bad things will happen—maybe you'll lose the relationship or look selfish—that isn't justice. It's just plain fear, and it's a trap.

And then there's a whole other category of people who go around 'doing good' to make themselves feel superior. They take a stray dog to the animal shelter, change a stranger's flat tire and give a panhandler their last $5, all on the way to work in the morning. When they help you, they aren't really worrying about you at all. They're using you to boost their own self-image.

Justice is something else entirely. Like the other virtues, justice always comes from deep thought and consideration. It isn't a knee-jerk emotional reaction to a fear that you'll lose a friendship or that your someone will be disappointed in you. If justice were a feeling, it would be more like gratitude: you're grateful for the people around you, and so you treat them fairly.

Question: It was easier for me to focus on the first part of the book when you were talking about sins. It felt like vital information that I could use. I'm having a hard time focusing on the virtues. Why is that?

Most people love to hear about the bad stuff in life—crime, accidents, screw-ups—because it's more exciting. Why do you think a murder gets more media attention than a nursing home that found a creative way to keep their Alzheimer's patients safe and happy? Why are people more likely to share posts about a celebrity divorce than about a couple that's been together for fifty years? Because they enjoy it. Sin is fun to think about, and it's fun to talk about.

I've always had a hard time getting my head around people's interest in sin, because I don't like talking about it. I teach about sin because I want people to see how it holds them back, but I don't find it exciting or interesting. In fact, I'd rather talk about almost anything else in the world.

That eager attitude about sin starts in school. Kids fall into bad habits when they're in large groups and there aren't enough strong, courageous adults around to correct them. Teachers don't have time to focus on the way their students treat each other, and parents are tired and distracted at the end of the day. So, moral education is the thing we let slide.

If you're having a hard time focusing on what it means to be a virtuous person, it's because you aren't used to thinking about it. Nobody talks about these things, do they? How are you supposed to concentrate on the virtues when you have so little experience with them? Sin is exciting. Temptation is easy. Virtue is work.

When I work with a client for months on end and tell them exactly what to do and what not to do, what music to listen to and what music to stay away from, their faith wakes up and they start to feel joy and a desire to show justice to the people around them. The change is obvious. They feel it. Things start to work out for them. But as soon as they try to do it on their own, they stumble. They go back to the ways of the world that they're used to, where everything is run by anger, envy, and pride. And the next time I see them, they almost all say the same exact words: "I need to express my individuality." That sounds good, doesn't it? What's wrong with expressing your individuality? But here's the thing: when they say that, it's actually their sins talking. Being virtuous is too hard when I'm not around to hold their hand. Sin is so much easier.

Question: Do we have to work on practicing justice with ourselves? For example, if I realise I made a serious mistake and punish myself for it, would that be right or wrong?

There's a big difference between punishing yourself, which is pointless, and repenting, which is good and useful. If you realise that you did something really wrong, you're supposed to repent, which can look different depending on what happened and whether or not you're religious. If you go to a church that practices repentance, you can talk to your priest and repent formally. Otherwise, you can do much the same thing at home by listing your sins on paper so you can see them in black and white. Then you promise whatever higher power you believe in that you will try to do better. It's that simple. There's no need for harsh punishment. You aren't the judge of anyone, either yourself or others.

Question: Can you explain more about why punishment isn't the answer?

No matter what happens, no matter how unfair life seems, the only person you can blame is yourself. And you shouldn't try to punish yourself, either. Life already punishes you for the bad things you do. Don't try to make it worse. You can confess what you did if that's relevant, repent, write in a journal, and promise yourself and God that you won't make the same mistake again. All of those are actions that can help you do better next time. Punishing yourself just digs your hole even deeper.

Question: Do you ever feel sad when you know you're doing the right thing? If you know you shouldn't try to hold on to a person and you let them go, is it alright to feel sad about that?

I know exactly what you're talking about. When I was younger, I experienced that kind of sadness all the time. It isn't a negative or angry kind of sorrow. It's just an acknowledgement that you can't do everything you want to do in this life. Some situations—and people—you have to walk away from. The next virtue we are going to look at is temperance, and one of the levels of temperance is patience. This is an incredibly important virtue, because the more you practice it, the less often you will feel sad about doing what you know is right.

Temperance

Now that you understand the meaning of justice and why revenge and punishment are always wrong, we can start talking about temperance. Long before I even knew the word temperance, I was telling my readers that living by your heart doesn't mean living without rules or without any form of self-control.

I had readers coming to me and saying, "I chose this path with my heart, but I'm getting slammed at every step." When I ask, "How do you know you chose it with your heart?" they almost always say, "Well, it's what I wanted to do." Friends, living by your heart is not the same as doing whatever you want to do at the moment. I'm not a proponent of free love. You have to check yourself and make sure that your heart is tuned to the right frequency before you trust your desires. That's temperance. Most people think of temperance in physical terms: you shouldn't eat or drink too much, but that's a shallow understanding. In reality, temperance means being able to control your desires. You control *what* you eat, not just *how much*. You control *who* you hang out with. You control *what* you want in your professional and social lives.

Temperance is the one thing that spiritual leaders and coaches leave out of their teachings, because everyone wants to hear about freedom, free love, and how there's nothing wrong with taking drugs to expand your mind. But as a matter of fact, temperance is the most important pillar of spirituality and spiritual development. When you practice temperance, you know the rules and you're on the lookout for temptation. Patience is a big part of it.

I've always been guided by temperance in my life, even before I knew what it was called. It was never something that my parents or teachers put a lot of emphasis on, it's just part of who I am. Temperance is not a life hack or a cute quote you can hang on the wall in your dining room. It's a daily practice that brings true spiritual growth. And my goal with this book is to help you put temperance in a central place in your life.

Here's a practical example of temperance in action: let's say someone gives you a large sum of money. It's enough to buy almost any car you can think of, or a home in some exotic location. But temperance tells you that you already have a good enough place to live and a good enough car, so you wait. You set aside that money and wait for a use that will truly benefit you and the people you care about. If you spend the money, you do it in a way that feeds your virtues instead of firing up your sins.

I get it: you think temperance is a drag. Letting sin drive your actions is always easier. I'm here to lay out all the cards and show you how the world works, but it's up to you to choose to read and follow the information I'm giving you.

In philosophy and Christian theology, temperance is defined as self-control and moderation for the purpose of spiritual growth. This is the one virtue that you'll never understand as long as you're living for the sake of pleasure and entertainment. If you head off to a beach resort as soon as you get your annual bonus, you aren't practicing temperance. If you buy stuff to make yourself feel better, you aren't practicing temperance. All the people who travel, eat out, buy clothes, and post photos on Instagram are devoid of temperance. I believe that we are seeing the last days when people can get away with living without boundaries. Don't get me wrong: I'm not saying you can't ever take a vacation. You just have to practice self-control. If you've worked hard all year, go somewhere that you can rest and recharge. But don't go again in a month. Your temperance should tell you that there are better uses for that time and money.

Unfortunately, many people confuse dark desires with desires that come from God. And a lot of you are in debt because of that confusion. If you think about it, the entire credit card industry exists for one purpose: to allow you to have things now instead of waiting for them. It's bad for you to have access to that kind of spending power until you've reached a spiritual level where you know what you need and know how not to fire up your sins. But if you think about it, debt forces people to work. Without that outside stimulus, a lot of people would just sit around doing nothing. Instead, the need to pay off their debt forces people to get out of bed and work. So, debt is one way life punishes you for your sins.

What if you've already moved up a level? You've learned how to earn more money than you spend, but you aren't using it to create community and accomplish goals with the people around you, and that means you aren't going to continue to grow. Life can't punish you through debt because you already have more money than you need, so the next thing that's going to go is your health. You'll get sick and end up spending all that extra cash on doctors. That's another way life enforces its rules.

Why am I giving you these harsh examples? Because I want you to see how the qualities you have inside determine what happens to you. The people you meet and opportunities you see aren't random; they all depend on whether you're feeding your virtues or your sins. That should be a powerful incentive to grow, because as soon as you start to feed those positive qualities like temperance and justice, you'll see the world around you change in ways you couldn't have dreamed of. People will treat you differently.

When you live a truly spiritual life, you want fewer things. Your needs are simpler. But here's the catch: temperance is not an excuse for not working. You can't just lie around in a hammock all day and say, "I don't need to work. I'm practicing temperance." That won't cut it. You have to be useful to yourself and your community. Remember how we talked about useful work in the section on greed? People who dream of lazing around on the beach and earning passive income aren't practicing temperance. They're depriving their community of useful work. They're greedy. So, don't use temperance as an excuse, because it isn't about working less; it's about buying less stuff and spending less time on social media. I'm not giving you this information so you can find a loophole for your sinful mind. Quite the opposite: I want you to live the truest life possible.

Questions and Answers about Temperance

Question: I'm reading along about sin and virtue and starting to feel like once you give me the tools to get started changing, it's going to be a lot of work. What advice do you have for those of us who are just now realising that life isn't about enjoying yourself and having a good time? Is this going to be too hard for me?

You're on the right track to be thinking about what it means to have desires and how those desires might change when you pursue spiritual growth. But let me ask you a question: if you look back on the past five to ten years of your life, can you honestly say that you were truly happy? Were you really enjoying yourself? Or were you always looking forward to things and thinking you would be happy when this or that happened or when you reached some goal or other? Because even though people tend to be attached to their desires, those desires are not what make us genuinely happy. They keep you running away from problems and toward something that you can't see even clearly. And your problems always seem to catch up to you at the end of the day. You never get to relax.

That's how people live when they make desire and enjoyment the central purpose of their lives. See how it doesn't work?

When I first started making videos, people would interview me and ask me how I was able to earn as much money as I did. I was just starting out, and people couldn't understand where all that success came from. My answer was simple: I was able to do it because my goal was not to achieve financial success. I didn't want to buy expensive clothes and cars. I didn't have a bucket list of exotic places I wanted to visit. None of that stuff mattered to me. It still doesn't.

By the way, don't listen to people who justify travel by saying that it expands your horizons. Sure, it can do that, but most people travel to get away from themselves and their responsibilities, not to immerse themselves in another culture. There has to be a goal to your travel, something with a higher meaning than sitting on the beach and sipping exotic drinks.

I strayed from your question a little bit, but I wanted to make it clear that a lot of the things people think of as pleasures don't really make you happy. You said you're worried about giving up things you enjoy in order to grow spiritually. But as you can see, true joy comes from developing your virtues. A genuinely happy person doesn't need to check off a list of countries they've visited. They don't feel empty inside, even when they do the same things every day. When you're happy, you see the everyday world in such a range of colours that you don't need the distractions that people call pleasures. The people who are enjoying their lives and doing amazing things didn't get there by reading books about how to be successful or by taking business classes. And they aren't motivated by greed. No, their secret is that they let themselves be led by their virtues.

Once you're led by your virtues, you'll find that your doubts melt away and life starts to look so much more hopeful. If your big idea is making the perfect carry-on bag, you read and find people to learn from. You sketch your ideas. You sell whatever you can sell—even your car—to pay for production samples. And all because you love your idea and believe in it.

But you have to be careful. If you let yourself get sucked back into society's values, you'll care more about what other people are doing than what you're doing. You'll start wanting things instead of achieving things. You'll lose sight of your goals, and you'll lose your confidence.

You asked if letting the seven virtues drive your life would be too hard. I don't think so. Not if you look at the alternative.

I won't lie to you: when you've lived by the rules of sin your entire life, you're going to have setbacks when you turn to virtue. But that's not life punishing you. Don't be mistaken. Those things that feel like losses are the price of your freedom.

If your significant other is still driven by sin, then all of a sudden you are going to see them in a different light. You may wonder how you could even have been with that person. But just as your mind is made of seven parts, or sins, your heart is made of seven parts, or virtues. And your virtues will make you happier than anything your sins ever promised. So be prepared for change, but don't be scared. The journey is absolutely worth it.

Question: I understand what you're saying about temperance, but if I cut all the pleasures out of my life won't I just want them even more?

Everybody thinks that, but it isn't true. Limiting yourself through virtue is not the same as someone else limiting you and not letting you do something you want. When you feed your virtues, you'll experience a whole new life. You won't want to go back to the old way of living even if someone paid you.

Think about people who give up smoking and junk food and start eating right and drinking water and exercising. It's hard for a week or two, but then you feel so much better that you can't imagine going back to the way you were. Your virtues work the same way. Once you get a taste of the confidence, freedom, and pure joy that come with virtues like temperance, you won't want to go back.

Question: You talk about practicing temperance and doing useful work, but I work all the time and still don't have any money for the things I want to do. What makes it hurt worse is that a friend of mine who never gives a thought about other people has way more money than I do.

This is one of the questions people ask me most often: why is this person or that person doing better than me financially? Here's the short answer: stop using money as the universal measuring stick.

For the long answer, I'm going to ask you to think logically: if you're having these jealous thoughts about your friend's success, where are those thoughts coming from? They're coming straight from your sins. Greed, envy, and pride are what make you compare yourself to others. Virtuous people don't think about money first thing when they wake up in the morning. They don't think about money when they see their friends buying things they themselves can't afford. This is important enough that it bears repeating: don't think about money. Let money come to you, and spend it when you need to. Otherwise, don't give it a thought.

That's one part of the answer. The other part of the answer is patience. You're probably still working at a job that you chose when you were driven by sin. Maybe that's why your hard work isn't rewarding you financially. Give yourself some time to make new, virtuous choices.

There could be other reasons you're working hard and not reaping material rewards but those are the first two that come to mind: your sins are still strong, and you're still in a situation that you chose before you started your journey toward personal growth.

Question: Is it bad to be a workaholic?

Of course. Any extremism is always bad for you. Helping people locate that line between normal activity and extremism was always hard for me, but once I started looking at the issue through the framework of sins and virtues, it suddenly became clear.

As soon as your virtues are driving your actions, you'll see right away when you should stop working and when you should keep going. The instant you do something that doesn't align with your soul, you'll feel it. You'll feel the emptiness inside, but the good news is that you'll be able to do something about it. Think of it as a natural preservation instinct for your soul.

I can work 24 hours a day sometimes. There were a few times recently where I felt like I was working too hard and pulled back to rest. Everyone is different in terms of how much they can work and when they need to take a break. What's important is that you learn to feel your own need for rest. Whether you're working or out having a good time, your virtues keep you aware of what's going on and let you know when you need to make a change.

Question: Is temperance related to modesty?

The two concepts are related, but you don't want to confuse them. When a person practices temperance toward the world around them, they don't want or need much. From the outside, that can look like modesty or humility. People think, "What a humble guy he is!" when in fact it's temperance.

After all, you can be modest and still be driven by sin. Think about that for a minute. Plenty of people act humble and shy for negative reasons. Maybe they lack confidence and they're afraid to speak up. Maybe they look down on the people around them and are too proud to socialize. Maybe they're depressed. There are plenty of explanations for why a person might be behaving modestly in certain circumstances. I'm being picky here, but I want you to see the difference.

Most of the time, though, modesty is a good thing. When I work with proud people whose egos are out of control, I always tell them to shut their mouths and learn to listen. Don't try to be first. Let other people have what they want. Keep your ideas to yourself. Learn to be a follower. If you keep insisting on having your own way, life will eventually bring you down a notch or two.

Honestly, it's hard to get people to take this advice. Everyone really wants to get their own way and push to the head of the line.

Modesty shouldn't come from a lack of confidence or any kind of pride. You should be able to speak up and ask for what you want directly because you know that your desires are guided by your temperance. In other words, if you ask for something, you should know it's the right thing to ask for and the right time to ask for it.

Here's another benefit to feeding your positive qualities: once you're driven by virtue, you'll feel more confident around people in work and social situations. You'll know what you're worth and you won't feel like you have to beg for recognition and acknowledgment. Negotiating becomes easier—not harder—when your actions are powered by virtue instead of sin. In fact, I can't think of a single situation where virtues like temperance *wouldn't* put you in a stronger position.

Question: Isn't moderation something that children are supposed to learn from their parents?

One hundred per cent. It's parents' job to raise their children to practice temperance in everything. But here's the problem: those same parents are always messaging me and wanting to know how they're supposed to do the job. Most are terrified that they're doing it wrong and ruining their children's lives. I always tell them you have to whip your kids until they're 18, but that gets me called a sadist!

Obviously, I'm not speaking literally. But you do have to tame your child and create a family system built on respect for the parents. If you fail to do that, the internet is waiting on your kid's device to teach them all about disrespect and materialism. It's much easier to curb a child's desires from the start than to fight those sins once they've had a chance to grow.

I know parents who think that if they love their children, they should let them do whatever they want. This can look appealing from the outside, and it certainly looks like less work, but the consequences for the child will be serious.

So, use the moral and practical power you have over your child as long as they are a minor. Teach them the lessons you want them to learn. Then when they reach 18—or 16 if they're a quick learner like a lot of kids are these days—get out of the way. Give them opportunities to get out into the world on their own and use what they've learned. They'll realise pretty quickly that temperance is one of the most important skills you could have given them. When I talk to young people, I see right away whose parents brought them up with self-control and whose let them run loose.

Question: How can I achieve temperance in my professional life? I have a hard time finding balance between working on projects and enjoying some downtime so I can recharge.

It depends on how hard you're working. There are plenty of people who 'work' 40-50 hours a week without getting much done. Their brains are in vacation mode when they're sitting at their jobs. And there are other people who never stop hustling and are at risk of burning out.

So, achieving balance can look different for different people. Pay attention to how productive you are at work and in your personal life. If you're focusing and meeting targets at work, then schedule some downtime for yourself. But if you're one of those people who has trouble focusing on work, then do the opposite: force yourself to work harder. Discover what it feels like to be really tired. Then let yourself rest. That's the only way you can find balance.

Question: Did the world's religions come up with the idea of fasting as a way to teach people temperance in their eating habits?

Absolutely. Most people overeat or reach for unhealthy foods to numb the spiritual pain that comes from living in a sinful world. We all have choices, including what we eat, and unfortunately we tend to choose wrong because we think that our favourite comfort food will make us feel better.

Fasts are like holidays or any other religious ritual. They were designed to keep people in touch with their spiritual lives and with God. They feed our temperance and keep us from losing our inner light. Since we aren't born with temperance, we have to learn it from our parents and practice it by adhering to rituals that include things like fasting.

Question: Can temperance help with loneliness?

If by loneliness you mean being alone for extended periods of time—not just the loneliness that follows a breakup or the like—then that is definitely an extreme situation. Temperance tells you not to be alone for weeks at a time, but it also tells you not to be on your phone or hanging out with friends all the time, too.

When I work with someone who spends every waking moment with friends or family, whether in person or via messaging, I tell them to take a day or two to be alone. It's good for them to turn off the constant conversations and listen to their own thoughts for a while. Conversely, I tell people who spend too much time alone to open up their time to loved ones.

For me, balance doesn't look like a 50-50 split between being alone and being with people. I just pay attention to my needs. When I need solitude, that's what I choose. I can stay by myself for days or weeks at a time. But when I need to, I can live and work in close contact with people for days or weeks at a time, too. I'm not rationing my time. I'm just avoiding extremes.

I wonder if you asked about loneliness because you feel yourself drawn to that extreme. In my lectures and classes, I do talk more about spending time alone because so many people are pulled in the other direction toward excessive socializing. But if you feel like your problem is too much time alone, then think of it this way: we need time alone so we can listen to ourselves, but we also need time with people so we can build on what we learn in that alone time and create rewarding relationships.

Question: Can you explain why you only use the internet when absolutely necessary?

Scrolling, surfing, browsing, cruising: those are all synonyms for wasting time. I don't go online unless I have a good reason, like teaching a class online or looking for information. If I want to find out the size of the biggest skull ever measured, I'll jump on, google it, and jump right back off. If I'm looking for a service provider, I'll check out the recommendations on social media. That's it.

Most people waste time online—looking at photos of other people's lives, doom scrolling through the news, reading and passing on rumours—because they've neglected to build lives of their own. And so, they're addicted to finding out what other people are doing. When you aren't busy with your own life, your brain is going to be desperately searching for something it can think about. And social media offers the perfect solution: just sit and scroll, sit and scroll.

Start learning temperance by cutting back on your internet and social media usage. Promise yourself that you will only look at social media on a certain day of the week. Restrict your general internet usage to when you really need to communicate with someone or find information. When you find yourself scrolling aimlessly, walk away from your device and do something else. Temperance says it's fine to use the internet to meet real needs, not to waste time.

Fighting an internet addiction is like losing weight. The point of going on a diet is not so that you'll look better in photos. The point is to learn to control your desires and motivation. Anyone who successfully loses a lot of weight will be strong enough to handle anything that comes their way. The same is true of getting off your phone. If you can put it down—and keep putting it down—you'll feed strengths and virtues that will put you on the path to success.

Question: Once I reach a certain level of temperance, will I be able to see the temptations around me for what they are?

Definitely. Once your temperance is strong, it will act like a powerful form of intuition that will show you all the hidden temptations. You'll be able to feel when you're in danger of feeding your egoism or greed. You'll naturally gravitate toward choices that feed your soul without looking impolite or insensitive.

But I have to warn you about a dangerous paradox: when your virtues are strong and your sins are losing their grip on your heart, that's when you'll be tested. Here's an example. Imagine a woman who spent the past two years trying to find a husband, but she's finally realised that she can't live her life that way. She has gotten past the stage of trying not to think about marriage. She's already at the level where she set down that burden and feels lighter. She doesn't care about externalities anymore. She's found her inner light and is building it up. Guess what? This is the point at which her ex-boyfriend will show up wanting to talk commitment. Or she'll meet the someone who looks like the man of her dreams and he's interested in her.

What's going on? She just gave up thinking about marriage, and here it is back on her radar. But it's just a trap. If she gives in to the ex-boyfriend or responds to the 'man of her dreams,' she'll lose everything.

The same thing can happen in your work life. Say, you've been freelancing for a few years and you just put a client on your blacklist because he's always coming to you with these projects that end up being a waste of your time. Maybe he's a little bit of a scammer, too. It took you a while to screw up your courage and tell him no, but you know it's the right thing to do. Well, no sooner do you put him on your brand-new blacklist than he comes to you with a project that has a huge budget and the client is ready to pay upfront. If you give in, you'll be right back where you started: under the influence of a shifty, dishonest person who has led you wrong before.

Those are the kinds of temptations you can expect to face as you begin to work on your virtues. A sudden wave of temptations is a good sign that you're moving in the right direction. That juts confirms that the system is working the way we know it does.

If you pass up those temptations, it won't take long before magical things start to happen in your life. Maybe you're a painter, and you've always struggled to get people to even look at your work. Once your life is driven by virtue, you'll start getting calls from galleries that want to buy from you. The effects will look different depending on what you're trying to achieve, but you'll notice it. I noticed these effects when I left home and started making my way in the world at seventeen. This is what I wrote my first book about. If your soul is open and pure, wonderful things will come your way. If it's closed—meaning that your sins are driving you—then you'd be safer staying home, because life will be out to teach you a lesson.

Not long ago, I watched the 2015 animated version of *The Little Prince*, and the director did a great job of showing the power of being on the right frequency. The little girl in the story has a mother who is cruel and materialistic, and she's raising her daughter to be the same way. But their neighbour is a lonely old man with all kinds of cool things in his house, everything from maps and globes to telescopes and old books. When he shows the little girl a few pages of Saint-Exupery's story about the little prince, she rejects it right away because it doesn't 'make sense.' She uses her closed mind to try to understand the story. Eventually, she understands the old man's world and is able to join him on the same frequency.

Most people in the world are on the same frequency as that little girl, and they react to my books the same way. But I just keep sharing the source of my joy with people through my books and classes, and when people find my content useful and pay me for it, I just put that money back into sharing more content so more people can know the source of that joy. My whole life is about sharing the magic that can be yours if you live by your heart and let your virtues be in charge. Seeing temptations for what they really are is just one of the benefits you'll find.

Question: Whenever I hear the words 'moderation' and 'temperance,' I picture people who work out all the time, abstain from drinking alcohol, and eat a plant-based diet. Do I have to completely overhaul my lifestyle to practice temperance as a virtue?

I'm not interested in your grocery list or how often you work out. Diets and workout programs have nothing to do with real virtue. It's hard to get to the frequency I call Peace, but once you're there, you'll see that the kind of rules you're used to just don't exist. Your virtues will keep you on the right track, so you won't need a list of approved foods or a list of workout routines you have to follow. If you're hungry, you'll eat. You'll be in tune with what your body needs instead of scrolling through some diet website to find out what foods are supposedly good for you.

So, the answer is no: you don't have to reach a certain body mass index or eat a specific diet to benefit from the virtue of temperance.

Question: What is the difference between hobbies and empty entertainment?

People who live by their hearts always have hobbies that they come to without being influenced by other people. They just choose something they love and get busy doing it.

A few years ago, I wrote a book where I talked about the power of crystals and minerals. If all my readers ran out and started collecting crystals, I wouldn't consider that a positive hobby, because they would just be copying an idea they read somewhere. For a hobby to be a positive force in your life, it has to come from your heart. Maybe it's something you learned from a grandparent or parent. Or something you've loved since you were a kid. The best hobbies are the ones where you find yourself in the zone, creating and meditating simultaneously.

Entertainment is different. People who are addicted to entertainment want to zip around on jet skis or motorcycles. Parasailing. Hang gliding. Loud concerts. Anything that gets your adrenaline pumped up. Anything that everyone else wants to do, too. Entertainment is when you want to play around without focusing your attention. You want people and noise and music. Entertainment wears me out. But when you're driven by sin, entertainment is exactly what you want.

Question: What do you think about Aristotle's teaching that moderation is the middle road between too little and too much?

Let's look at an example of 'too much' in a modern context. Think of the people you know who share every single detail of their lives on social media. If they have a thought, they share it. If they buy something, they share it. Nothing is secret from their followers. They don't have a private life.

Privacy is one of the most important aspects of the Peace frequency I teach about. A place where you can sit and have dreams you don't share with anyone. Your private thoughts are too valuable to spread all over the internet. The places that delight you are too important to tag for all your friends to see.

I used to make the same mistakes online, oversharing and posting about all my favourite creators and places to go. In my defence, I wasn't trying to leverage the attention economy. I was just eager to show my readers all the wonderful people and places I was discovering. But eventually, I realised that all that oversharing took away from my own private life. Everyone needs to have secrets, things that only you know about. The things you don't talk about and don't show to the whole world are the things that feed your inner fire. Keep your favourite places, songs, and people to yourself. Enjoy them without feeling the need to tell the whole world about them. In the modern attention economy, the world pushes you to share-share-share. Social media would die without our content. But when you share something online, you cheapen it for yourself.

Here's another angle on the same issue: if I write a song and personally share it with you and you turn around and post it to your Instagram feed, then you've cheapened my song and you've cheapened our relationship. Think before you share things, and make sure you aren't wasting things that matter to you just to get some stranger's attention.

Sexual promiscuity is an obvious example of 'too much,' of being reckless with your body, but people are also reckless with their belongings. Think of all the kids whose parents give them everything they want. They have a nice car, but they let their friends drive it around and wreck it. They have a beach condo, but they let random strangers wander into their parties and pretty soon the place looks like a dump. They loan their laptop to someone and forget who has it. That's a form of recklessness I see in kids from rich families.

Temperance is the answer to all these extremes of too much sharing, and it will help you decide who you want in your private life and who needs to stay on the outside.

Question: Do you ever feel tempted to throw moderation out the window? If so, what do you do to stay on track?

Not anymore. Had you asked me that question four or five years ago, I would have said that yes, I was tempted to overshare or overeat or otherwise overdo things. But that was when I lived in the world. In 2012, I decided to live in the world and learn about all the sins you could possibly have. I called it studying the material world. My most important rule during that time was that I didn't want to lose myself. No matter how far I went with the experiment, I wanted to stay true to myself.

But I did lose sight of moderation. When you live by the laws of the world, you have a harder time seeing the line that you aren't supposed to cross. The hardest thing for me in that respect was finding moderation in my social life. My girlfriend at the time had a large family, and it was a normal thing for them to celebrate someone's birthday for a whole week, complete with out-of-town guests. When you get caught up in a house party that spills over into a big family road trip, it's hard to find time to be alone with your thoughts. I found that I was taking on the sins of the people I was socialising with.

I have help from above, though. As soon as I get distracted by sin, punishment arrives immediately. Same-day delivery. So, for the past four years, I have had no desire to walk away from temperance. There have been a few times that I've worked a little too much, but otherwise I practice moderation in everything.

Faith

I'm not going to give you my own definition of faith right now, because you probably already have some ideas of your own about what faith is. Instead, I want to show you why faith is one of the seven virtues and how it can help you improve your life. But first, take the time to write down your own thoughts about faith. Once you've got it fresh in your mind, keep reading.

When I first started writing books and teaching classes, there was one question that people asked me more than any other: "Why are you helping people? What are you getting out of it?" That was a hard question for me to answer, because there was this assumption that I stood to gain something, that I was making money or benefiting somehow, when in fact I just felt like being helpful. People who aren't driven by sin have a natural desire to be helpful without any particular reason. You don't do good deeds 'because,' you just do them.

But then people started asking me essentially the same question a different way: "Where do you get the inspiration from to keep writing and speaking?" That's a good question, because if the inspiration wasn't there, people would notice right away. My message wouldn't get through to them.

So, I started thinking about what moves me. Where do I get all my ideas from? And what it came down to was faith.

Sometimes, faith is easier to understand by looking at its opposite: doubt. Doubt is a terrible feeling that keeps you from believing in yourself. Your friend or your partner says, "Let's build a house together," or "Let's start a business," but your doubt makes you hesitant. It sucks the energy out of you. Faith, on the other hand, makes you so strong that you don't need physical or moral support from anyone.

That's why faith is one of the seven virtues. Actually, it's more like a superpower. And the stronger you can get it burning, the better. Here's why:

People come to me all the time with questions about motivation. They don't feel motivated to take on projects or learn new skills. They come up with a good idea, but then they get bored and drop it. There can be a lot of different reasons for this, but a lack of faith is one of the most common. When your seven virtues are strong—especially faith—then nothing will stop you. Not your family, not your finances, not the economy. Nothing.

If you are driven by sins like pride and greed, you need immediate gratification to keep working. When a project doesn't turn a profit right away, you lose interest. But if you're fuelled by faith, you'll be working for more than just worldly results, and you'll stay the course no matter what.

Questions and Answers about Faith

Questions: What kinds of feelings are created by faith?

When you have faith, you have a deep sense of never being alone. Some people have felt this way their whole lives and don't even know how special it is. Other people have never felt it. I'm alone in my room right now, but I know there is someone nearby, right above me. You don't have to assign that presence a gender. It's just an attentive presence that makes you feel full, never empty. Some people talk about being visited by the Holy Spirit. It's a higher power that enters your body. That's what I feel. That's what I call faith.

Faith helps you understand the world and your place in it. It's like waking up and seeing everything for the first time. That's the best way I can describe the feeling of faith.

In action, faith is like the other virtues we've talked about. When I make choices, I'm led by my faith, not by my mind. It's like being connected to God's own wi-fi. That means I don't have to analyse each situation in depth. I just have to honour that connection and go the direction it leads me. And if I don't feel led, I don't make a move. Faith gives me that freedom.

Faith tells me where to go, what to publish, what to edit out, what to sign, and what to negotiate. It's my superpower. It never leads me wrong.

Question: What is the difference between knowing something for sure and having faith?

There is no such thing as knowing something for sure. The world you see around you is an illusion. When I tell people how life works, there are always a few people who want me to explain the where, what, why, and how. And I always tell them it doesn't work that way. The minute I lay it all out for you, your mind will be satisfied, but I won't have made any progress toward opening your heart. You just have to believe me, come what may. Some people literally can't do it. They want to prepare for everything using their minds. They want to make choices using their minds. Because that's what they're used to. They've never had faith, so they rely on their minds for everything.

Fear is also a factor. People without faith fear so many things. They'd rather live without miracles than have to accept that there's something outside their understanding. And miracles can be scary. So, they drive the same route to work every day and eat the same thing for lunch every day. Their souls are closed off, and they can't grow. That's a bad way to live.

Do you see how different faith is from knowledge? Ninety-nine per cent of the time, knowledge will lead you in the wrong direction. And when life holds out its hand with an amazing chance, you'll turn it down because your mind will want to take the path of knowledge instead of the path of faith. When you think about it, knowledge doesn't seem all that valuable, does it?

Imagine a young man who wants to change his life. He reaches out to me, and he reaches out to a personal trainer who runs yoga retreats. Here's how I reply when people contact me wanting something different in life: "Come spend at least two days with me in Karelia, and be ready to spend the whole time learning. There won't be any downtime for you to sit around on your phone." I let them know that Karelia is full of mosquitos in the summer, and that my house is a plain, wooden building without running water. But if you want to change your life, it's the place to be.

Then the guy opens the email from the personal trainer, and it's full of links to beautiful people doing yoga in million-dollar yurts. They have an instructor who lived in India for ten years, and you can opt to take classes in esoterica and meditation for an extra fee. There's a detailed schedule for each day, and you can choose your meals ahead of time. Click the "Sign me up!" button and you're on your way to finding your truest inner self. The promises sound amazing.

If he chooses with his mind, the guy in my example will choose the yoga retreat every time because he knows exactly what will happen in thirty-minute increments. He knows what he'll eat for breakfast every day. The yoga retreat offers him knowledge and certainty. I'm asking him to have faith. When you choose with your mind, you'll choose wrong every time.

What about intuition, though? Do you feel like you make your choices based on some kind of instinct or sixth sense? Be careful with that. Most of the time you're just listening to your own desires. People are good at convincing themselves that what they want is what they ought to do. Everyone thinks they have all the virtues and none of the sin. They know it all.

In reality, it takes a lot of hard work to root out sin and build up virtue to the point that your faith leads you effortlessly in the right direction.

Question: How do people lose their faith?

People lose their faith when they stop listening to God. Faith means being tuned in to God. When you listen to the people around you or to your desires, that leads you away from faith. If my friend tells me to do something—even something small, like buying a new shirt or going out to dinner—that goes against the voice of my faith and I do it, then I've taken a step away from faith. If I feel called to take a certain job, but someone else in my life convinces me to take a different job instead, then I'm allowing my faith to weaken. If I'm an artist and I let my friends and family influence what I paint because they want me to sell more of my work, I lose a piece of my heart. Do you see how it works? Small things, big things: it doesn't matter. You have to choose with your heart every time. People with strong faith are absolutely fearless.

Remember that your faith is always in motion. It's either growing or dying based on the choices you make. Pursue your heart and your faith grows. Follow society like a robot and it dies.

Question: What about people who lose their faith after something bad happens to them?

The worst thing that can happen to a person of faith is to spend time with friends who don't have faith. When the messengers first came to me and I discovered how energy flows inside and between people, I told a close friend about it and he was just as euphoric as I was. We listened to classical music together and supported each other on our spiritual journeys.

But my other friends reacted differently. They tried to poke holes in my story because the things I took on faith scared them. When I told them about the messengers that came to me, they mocked me: "Were your messengers from outer space? Did they glow in the dark?" When I told them about the anomalous places I discovered in Karelia and the powerful way people reacted to those places, my materialistic friends kept coming up with materialistic explanations: "Maybe it was the fresh air. Or radiation. Whatever it was, it wasn't magic."

People with worldly minds stomp on every miracle they see. If you listen to people like that, they'll drag you down and kill your faith. You start to question what you felt and saw. Your mind starts to analyse what other explanations there might be.

I hope you see how important it is to surround yourself with faith in all its forms: make friends with people who live by their hearts, be virtuous in your actions, choose the physical reality of your life—where you live, what you wear, what music you listen to—in order to reinforce your faith.

If you family and friends don't support the work you are doing to strengthen your faith, then limit your contact with them for a while. Try to surround yourself with positive energy and good people so you can freely believe in miracles. Remember that your faith depends on your ability to tune out the opinions of non-believers. A person of faith derives so much joy from their inner life and close friendships that they don't have time to care what other people think. Without that faith, you start living to please the world around you. You're constantly afraid of being judged and rejected. Why does this happen? It's simple: when you have faith, God is the only judge of your life; when you don't have faith, that authority gets taken over by the people who surround you. You let mere mortals—people who struggle with their own fear and sin—tell you what to do.

A lot of young people hand over the authority in their lives when they head off to college. Imagine a young woman who always loved her family, felt confident about her looks, and didn't give a whole lot of thought to social class. She's had a stable, happy life. But as soon as she's on campus with thousands of young people from across the economic spectrum, she starts judging herself based on the world's standards. Instead of being grateful for what her parents can do for her, she feels deprived that she doesn't have all the material things—shoes, earbuds, phone, you name it—that she sees around her. She starts to feel embarrassed that her parents aren't rich and successful. Now, she's following beauty influencers instead of doing homework and wondering if she should try out something like 'Only Fans,' so she can afford the same bag her roommate has.

What a miserable waste of a life. When you play games with the devil, you're always afraid. You can't take a step without worrying what other people will think. Don't post that photo: what will your boss think? Don't wear that shirt: what will your friends say? Don't get that degree: what will your ex-girlfriend or ex-boyfriend say? Without faith, every single person who wanders through your life gets to judge you like God.

Faith frees you from all of that, because God becomes your only judge. You get to stop chasing after the world's changing definition of 'good enough.' You feel free to post photos of your actual life—eating lunch with your mom, hanging out at the playground with your neighbours' kids—and you aren't afraid of anyone laughing at you. It's the best kind of freedom.

Question: Will praying every day help me find faith?

No, it won't. If you are led by sin and fear and resentment in your daily life, no amount of prayer will help. Imagine a scale with all that sin on one side and a handful of prayers on the other side.

If you want to know what it is like to live in faith, you have to completely change your life. You have to stop watching depressing or violent movies and listening to angry music. You have to stop reacting to your family members with anger and bitterness. You have to stop being driven by fear and cowering in your comfort zone. Keep that image of a scale in your mind. Saying a prayer every day won't put enough weight on the good side of the scale. You have to work on lightening the bad side while you add good deeds and positive relationships to the good side. Faith is action. It's a choice you make with your heart.

And remember that all the virtues hold together like a web. If you haven't worked on moderation, courage, and justice, then it's too early for you to be thinking about faith. Focus on the other virtues and choose actions that reinforce them. After a while, you'll start to see faith unfold in your life. It happens on its own time.

Question: Is it possible to take faith to the extreme? I'm thinking of people who say they are fearless.

If someone tells me they can jump from a tenth-floor window and not get hurt, that isn't faith. It's insanity. They're letting their mind tell them what faith is. Having faith doesn't make you immortal or incapable of being pierced by any weapon. It just means you make choices with your heart. So, there is no extreme of faith.

Question: How do I tell faith from overconfidence?

If you've read this far, then you know that faith grows through living virtuously and letting God be the only judge of your life. But the world is full of shallow people who build up a facade of overconfidence based on sins like greed and pride. What they have isn't faith; it's an illusion of their own importance. True faith is without ego. It helps you live modestly, following your heart, allowing miracles to happen without being in charge.

What the sinful world calls 'confidence' has nothing to do with faith. It's an illusion of power. Overconfident people believe that they are in charge and that God is on their side. Is that surprising? Even materialistic people know how to claim divine guidance when it suits them. But it's a risky business. Go around waving the cross and you risk getting hit by a bus. Life doesn't like overconfident people.

True faith has a soft voice. It won't tell you that you're the most important person in the world. It won't tell you to go rock climbing without a rope. It won't make you think you can jump in front of a bullet without getting killed. The people that believe those stories don't have faith. They have a stupid degree of overconfidence.

There's a paradox inherent in faith that I want to warn you about. The more you live by faith and make choices with your heart, the more you'll see miracles happening in your life. But when you tell your friends and family about those miracles, the materialists among them will try to convince you that the explanation is something completely ordinary. Something that can be proven scientifically. Do you see the paradox? The more you believe, the more you'll hear disbelief from the people around you. Having more faith means encountering more doubt.

You'll also start seeing signs. When I bought my property in Karelia, it all came together almost without my help. It was like the wind picked up one day and blew me to the place I was supposed to be. Once you live by faith, you'll notice this feeling of being protected by a powerful force that sometimes supports you and sometimes stops you from doing certain things. It's not something that you do with your mind. You don't need to copy me or anyone else. You'll just feel that there's a force leading you in the right direction. That's God helping you and making you his helper. As long as you're driven by sin and fear, then there isn't much you can do for him. But the more you grow your faith, take care of your physical and spiritual health, and listen to him, the more likely it is that God will be able to use you.

God hasn't used me yet. I just write books for the handful of people who want to live better, happier lives. Materialistic people can't stand me. They think I'm a self-styled coach who makes money by misleading people. But here's the interesting thing: I'm not in a hurry. I'm not looking to be famous. When you are driven by virtue, you don't feel like you're always running out of time. The sinful people are always rushing around in a panic, but I have plenty of time. Instead, what I'm focused on is growth. When I want to write, I write. If I stop wanting to write, I might not come back to it for years. But that's okay. I believe in serendipity.

It was serendipity that brought you to read this book, wasn't it? Millions of people listen to rappers glorifying their own body parts and the drugs they smoke. My readership might just be in the thousands. But again, that's okay. I don't mind being part of the less popular underground. If I was famous, I wouldn't have as much time to think and write. As it is, I know that the people who need me will find me. And if you get tired of this book, you can put it down and go back to your regular life. Eventually, someone else will hear about it and pick it up. That's exactly the space I want to be in.

Question: Are there different levels of faith? Can a person's faith grow over time?

That's a big topic. My faith is strong compared to most people's, but there have been periods when I felt its limits. Those limits show me how much I've grown and how much I still need to grow. Three years ago, the boundary was in a different place. My faith is a thousand times stronger now, but I can still see some limits.

How do I know? When I disappoint myself. For example, I spoke with the voice that knows everything, and I asked it, "Can I show people a miracle?" And it said, "You can." But my faith wasn't big enough to make a miracle happen. When it's storming outside, I could point at a tree and ask God—or the angels, or aliens, whatever you want to call the higher power—to hurl a lightning bolt into it. I can make that request. And the higher power hears me and can fulfil my request. But it doesn't, because my faith is still too weak. Think about it: if a lightning bolt hits the tree I'm pointing at, I'm going to wet my pants. My loved ones will be terrified. They're already a little afraid of the force that drives me, and a burned-up tree would send them over the edge. It would be mayhem. So, my faith isn't strong enough for visible miracles. I can't quite believe that God would answer my prayer in such an immediate way. That's the limit of my faith. That's where my doubts creep in.

The miracles that have happened to me have been unexpected. I believe in God, but not 100%. I don't want to tell lies or be egotistical. I don't want to be selfish. I may not have enough faith to work obvious miracles, but I have enough faith to be scared of sin. I believe in a higher power, in God, and I believe that he will punish me if I get out of line. If I end up on the street without any money or friends, my faith tells me that God will keep me safe. I live a clean life and haven't done anything to deserve punishment. But the next step of faith is miracles, and I'm not there yet. That's how I understand the levels of faith.

Question: How does faith affect the choices people make?

Faith has a pervasive effect on every choice you make. About a month ago, a new member of my staff came to me with some ideas for how I could get some publicity. He was trying to be helpful, but I had to remind him that I'm not here to get a huge following. If that was my goal, I'd put out short videos with clickbait titles on topics people actually want to hear about. I'd design an attractive website with a big call-to-action button for classes and retreats. Sign up today! Only three seats left! But I'm not here to excite people. And I don't want a bunch of followers who aren't interested in my real message. If someone wants the information I share, they'll find my books and read them. They'll put up with my slow-paced videos.

When you choose to listen to me, you're choosing based on faith. No one designed the experience that brought you here. You didn't pick the prettiest cover. You chose my message because you believed that I had something valuable to say. And I thank you for that.

Hope

If you struggle with despair, hope will be your most important virtue. Having hope means believing that better times are coming, no matter what is happening in your life today. Let's say, you're trying to accomplish something—maybe you want to find a new job, start a family, or reach a professional goal—and it isn't working out the way you wanted. There are obstacles everywhere you turn. What happens if you don't have hope? You give up. You stop writing your book or taking photos. You stop interviewing for better jobs. You just put your head in your hands and say, "I give up, it won't work." Hope is what tells you that everything will turn out fine in the end, even if you can't see that end yet.

I can think of a million examples of how hope changes our reactions to situations in daily life, but the true value of hope runs even deeper. When you have hope, you expect everything to work out perfectly, even if it isn't what you expected. Without hope, you find yourself on the path to depression and despair. No matter where you live, how much money you have, or how much of a support network you have, hope is the one thing that keeps you deeply engaged and loving your life. Losing that hope is the worst thing that can happen to you.

Questions and Answers about Hope

Question: How is faith different from hope?

Faith is about being led by a higher power and making choices using the instincts that come from being tuned into that higher power. Hope is a deep sense that everything will be okay, even if your plans aren't working out the way you wanted.

Question: What kinds of choices feed hope and make it stronger?

Even though I have a strong sense of how the virtues are all interconnected and how they reinforce each other, I can't give you a simple recipe for cultivating hope. The sins and the virtues are all a part of living nature, and it's hard to reduce that complexity down to a black and white recipe.

Let's look at it logically, though. If you keep away from actions that reinforce your sins and try to make virtuous choices, then it makes sense that you will notice hope starting to take root in your heart. You can feed that hope by choosing to live a moral life and cultivating the joys of your heart instead of the joys of the world, avoiding greed and egotism.

But don't forget that all the virtues are linked. If I didn't have faith, where would I get my hope from? That's how I understand it. To have hope, you first need faith. And in order to find faith, you first have to cleanse your heart of sin and turn on positive traits like temperance and fortitude. Doing those things will create a link between your heart and a higher power, and you'll understand your own inner life and what you need to thrive. The more you pay attention to that link, the stronger you will become.

When I first started writing, I talked about people being closed or open. Closed people never see miracles. They don't like to talk about deep feelings. They aren't interested in the teachings I share. But then something happens, some life-changing accident or death in the family, and they realise that they need to talk to someone about the deeper, truer side of life. That's when they remember me and my books. Or maybe that's the first time they hear about me. I call that time of change in a person's life 'the Corridor,' because it leads them to my teachings. When a person is closed off, their attention is focused on the world of work, school, and daily life. But then something shakes up their world and frees up their attention so they can look deeper and see how sin and virtue affect what happens to them. They start to wonder what their life could look like if they didn't waste their time in nightclubs. What might happen if they read a book or spent an evening with their parents? They might eventually make their way to one of my books and gain some true insight into how to live well.

I've had so many people come to me after a consultation or a class and tell me that they can see clearly now and they're going to live a different life. Sadly, most turn around and go right back to all the same sins that caused their problems in the first place. Why? Because they return to the same friend groups and the same ways of spending their free time. Those influences are strong. You can end up being two different people: one under the influence of sin and another under the influence of virtue.

Question: Is it enough to hope for something, or do I have to actively try to make it happen?

Questions like this tend to come from a place of greed or fear. The passive hope you describe is generated by the mind, not the heart. The seven virtues can never hurt you. They'll never make you lazy or careless. There's nothing virtuous about thinking, "Now that I believe in God and have hope, then I can just lie around and wait for good things to come my way." Life has some hard lessons to teach people who think that. And remember that all the virtues work together as a strong foundation for your life. You can't have faith and hope without also practicing moderation.

Even more important, I want you to always remember that the seven virtues are feelings, not thoughts or plans. Your thoughts are generated by sin. When you have hope, you don't go around thinking, "I have hope, so I can accomplish this or that." You just feel the hope as a powerful internal support that's there when you need it.

So, hope isn't a get-out-of-work-free card that lets you plan what you want without working to achieve it. Be modest in what you wish for, and be willing to work for those desires. Let hope be your spiritual sustenance, not a ladder to climb.

Question: I'm having a hard time understanding how hope is supposed to be positive. My parents taught me not to hope for things. They always said, "Stop hoping and get out there and make it happen."

There is a big difference between hoping with your heart and wanting with your mind. Think of it this way: if you do nothing with your life, you aren't contributing to your community and you're at risk of falling prey to sin. Imagine a person who gets sick and doesn't bother going to the doctor. Or their roof springs a leak and they don't get up there and fix it. If you confront them, they'll say, "I *hoped* things would turn out. I *hoped* my back pain would go away. I *hoped* it would stop raining and the roof would stop leaking." What they're describing isn't hope. It's laziness or depression, maybe both.

Your parents were right about not waiting around for things to happen to you, but they were mistaken to call that hope. True hope is spiritual support. It has nothing to do with being lazy and unmotivated or expecting other people to do things for you. In fact, hope is what gives you the strength to work hard and never give up. Hope fuels you to work harder than you thought possible. It keeps you from giving up, even when you have to deal with unexpected obstacles. Because you know that as long as you do your best, everything will be okay. That's the power of hope.

Question: Is hope infectious? If I have hope in my heart, will the people around me grow hopeful, too?

Quite possibly. But you can't force your friends and family to have hope. You can't use a recipe to make it happen. It has to happen freely because they notice that you live a sincere, heartfelt life. They have to see it on their own.

When you make virtuous choices, those choices will influence your friends, relatives, and co-workers. And if your close friend or significant other comes to you with a problem, your hope will shine through in everything you say to them. You don't have to try to teach them to have hope, you just have to let your own hope shine through in the words you use. It's enough for them to feel your hope and start to think about it. They'll wonder what it would be like to have hope of their own. They'll understand that their problem isn't the end of the world.

Don't try to make it happen, though. If you think you can take your friend and teach them to have hope, then you still have sin you need to work on. Truly virtuous people aren't running around like superheroes saving everybody. If you look closely at a person who thinks they can be a saviour—for animals, children, the elderly, the homeless—you'll usually find that they're motivated by pride. Real hope will never turn you into a fanatic or a crusader.

But how do you turn on people's hope? Is it difficult to do?

People aren't machines. I can't reach into a person's chest and flip the switch labelled 'hope.' We're more like plants that need to be watered and cared for. Only instead of water, what we need is attention. When I work with a person, I pay close attention to them and support them while they figure out what virtue looks like in their life. In every situation that comes up, I tell them what choices to make and how to react. I give them a personalised playlist of movies to watch and music to listen to. But as soon as I back off and let them try to do it on their own, a lot of them start to stumble and fall into sin again. The reason? Because they go back to hanging out with the same friends and listening to the same music. They watch a horror movie. Or a neighbour comes over and wants to smoke a joint with them. It doesn't take much to lose all the progress they made. Before you know it, they're depressed again, worried about not having enough money or not having the right background for their dream job. Confidence and joy are what you stand to lose if you don't keep yourself on the path of virtue. Why would you give that up?

Question: Is it okay to have hope that my parents or friends will be there to help me when I have problems?

You still don't understand what hope really is. Waiting around for someone—whether a parent or a friend—to fix your problems isn't hope. It's just a form of laziness that people like to call 'hope.'

Hope has nothing to do with your expectations of other people. Here's an example: if I didn't have true hope in my life, I'd be plagued by doubt all the time. I'd have a negative outlook on life. I wouldn't believe in myself. I'd think, "I've written ten books now and I'm still not famous. I must be a real loser." That would be problem number one. Problem number two would be comparisons: I'd continually compare myself to others. Look at how successful Dave Ramsey and Brene Brown are; their books come out in print runs that are a thousand times larger than mine. I must not be a real writer. Or look at that guy on TikTok who published three books already. He has three times more followers than I do. I must not be a real writer. That's how people think when they don't have hope and are led by the world's values.

If I listened to doubt and compared myself to others all the time, pretty soon I would want to give up. Remember how I said that a long time ago some messengers appeared in my life and told me I'd been chosen? Well, if I didn't have hope, I'd look around and decide that some millionaire IT entrepreneur looks a lot more 'chosen' than me. After all, I'm just a regular guy with back trouble and a goofy laugh. Who am I to teach classes and write books telling people how to get more joy and fulfilment out of life? That's what life is like when you don't have hope.

Comparison eats away at your soul 24 hours a day. It tears down your confidence and your relationships. If you're married, you start to look around and notice that other people's husbands or wives make more money or are in better shape than yours. Your friend's children all play musical instruments, but your kid just wants to ride their bike up and down the street. Other families vacation in Europe, but your family goes to your in-laws' lake house every summer.

So, you can see that hope has nothing to do with other people and everything to do with how you view your own life.

Question: Why do people always list faith, hope, and love together?

There's a reason why faith, hope, and love are like three sisters. They are all linked by one word: meaning. When you understand the meaning of life, you know there is a higher power above you. You understand that God created the world and that nothing is meaningless. That's faith. And if life isn't empty and random, then you have hope that your life has meaning. Do you see how these concepts are linked? And one you have that faith and that hope, you naturally love the world and all the people around you. All three words point back to that core concept of life having meaning.

Love

A lot of people in the personal growth space like to say things like, "love will save the world," or "God is love," or "learn to love yourself." And if you spend any time in church, you'll hear the phrase, "love your neighbour as yourself." Those are familiar takes on love, and I will not repeat them here. I want to get to the heart of what love means.

Shallow people think of love as a warm fuzzy feeling. You love Chinese food, you love your new car, you love your mom. Sure, you love your mom more than your new car, but they think it's essentially different degrees of the same emotion. You see someone you're attracted to and 'fall in love at first sight.'

That's how the world talks about love, but those concepts don't satisfy me. All the world's religions say that love is a powerful force, but when I look around, I see people falling in and out of love like it's no big deal. Today you love something and tomorrow you're over it. After thinking and reading, I realised that the word 'love' means something very different in philosophy and theology—the study of God—than it does in everyday life.

In the context of philosophy and theology, love means acceptance. Anywhere you see the word 'love,' just substitute in the word 'accept.' I accept myself. I accept the people around me.

But what is acceptance? When you accept the world, you avoid conflict. You don't go around arguing with people and trying to change their minds. You don't try to turn people to your way of thinking. You don't look at everything through the filter of your own sin. And why do you want to have that kind of acceptance for the world? Because it gives you freedom. Were you born poor? Do you have crooked teeth? Did someone steal something you worked hard to buy? When you accept the reality of your life, you don't react negatively to it. That's acceptance. That's love. And it's a real superpower: when you love and accept your life, nothing can upset you anymore. No matter what happens in your relationships with your family, friends, co-workers, or boss, you never feel angry. You hate no one. Don't get me wrong: you may still have to raise your voice and speak sharply sometimes to get your point across. But you won't be boiling over inside.

That doesn't mean that everyone with a good poker face loves you. Someone can smile politely at you while hating you inside. And if you judge people by their exterior, this kind of acting might fool you. The opposite is also true: someone who loves you dearly may on occasion need to tell you some things you don't want to hear. How do you tell who is really on your side and who is secretly against you? By how they behave over time. The person who loves you will always have your best interests in the front of their mind. The person who is just being polite to cover up how much they hate you won't miss a chance to hurt you and betray you.

So, in philosophical terms, loving someone means accepting them. When you have love in your heart, you accept and understand everything that happens. You might not even realise why you react so calmly to life. Maybe you think there's something wrong with you. You friends are always reminding you about the nasty things your ex-boyfriend or ex-girlfriend did to you, but none of it makes you mad. You accept your former significant other for who they are, you accept yourself, and you accept what happened.

This is a great place to be. You're as light as a feather. Nothing can knock you down. Let's imagine that you applied to college and didn't get in. You might call the admissions office to see if they would be willing to reconsider, but you don't get depressed or angry or ashamed. You think, "I'll be fine. This just means there's a better place out there for me."

Love in the form of acceptance makes family relationships a lot easier, too. I work with so many people who are still angry at their parents for mistakes they made decades ago. They ask me why I don't have any resentment against my own mom and dad. My answer is always, "Why would I?" My parents are just like everybody else. They're human. You have to stop looking at your parents as being special. See them as people just like you. They were born in a certain place and time and in a certain family. Maybe they were born into random families that weren't able to help them figure out who they are. Or maybe they were born in a neighbourhood with bad schools. They're just humans like you, with doubts and sorrows that keep them up at night. Maybe they harbour resentment against their own parents.

The highest level you can reach is when you stop judging and start loving and accepting everything and everyone. You know that God exists and that, even though you have to work and grow as a person, you're ultimately in the care of the Creator. When I go about my regular life, I feel the Creator's presence and know that he's aware of me, too. He's been guiding me for thirty years now, and he'll keep guiding me in the future. Because of that, I accept whatever comes my way. That's what I want for each of you: I want you start learning acceptance by accepting yourselves. Accept your aches and pains, your appearance, your strengths and weaknesses. All the things you like and dislike about yourself. Just accept them. As you reach the highest level of love, you'll start to feel the same about the people around you. Everything is the way it is for a reason. You can be deeply interested in life—the difficulties, the obstacles—without judging any of it.

The biblical definition of love is long, but it essentially says the same thing:

Love is patient and kind; love does not envy or boast; it is not arrogant or rude. It does not insist on its own way; it is not irritable or resentful; it does not rejoice at wrongdoing, but rejoices with the truth. ***Love bears all things, hopes all things, endures all things. Love never ends****.*
-I Corinthians 13, 4-7

If you look at the part of the definition in bold, you'll see that it lines up closely with what we have been talking about: accepting whatever happens.

Acceptance can be hard to get your head around. When a client complains about something bad that happened to them, I just smile and say, "That's life. It's supposed to be like that sometimes. It could be random, or it could be you're reaping the consequences of something you did." I remind them that when they let themselves be driven by sin, they attract negative consequences. Then I give them a little speech about how to move forward: *Now that this bad thing has happened, think back to your first reaction. What was your first thought? Follow that gut instinct. That is what the system needs you to do. The important thing to remember is that everyone you encounter in life was created by God, just like you were. Even if someone hurts you or does you wrong, you have to tell yourself that everything is fair and everything happens for a reason. Clean up your act and you won't attract negative, angry people into your life.*

"Love bears all things." It also bears all people. When you are filled with love and acceptance, you understand that all things are from God. All your negative experiences are given to you so you can grow. If you can't accept life the way it is, then you can't really love. You end up angry, constantly arguing, dissatisfied with God.

Christian writers also link love and mercy. A loving person is merciful. What does that mean? The way I understand it, showing mercy means having empathy, putting yourself in the other person's shoes. That's just another way of describing acceptance. There are plenty of anxious and angry people in this world, but the mercy of love tells you not to judge them. Accept them the way they are. Remember that nature is full of healing plants and poisonous plants. The same is true of people: some are kind and restorative, while others are out to do you harm. Here's another thing about love that is hard to get your head around: true love—the love that is synonymous with acceptance—is the same for everyone in your life. You can't love your mother more than you love your downstairs neighbour. This love is not a feeling of warmth and connection. It's not the physical attraction between lovers. It's just absolute acceptance.

It's a mistake to think that you can love your family and your friend group and not care about anyone outside that tiny circle. Most people categorise their relationships by level of importance. You'll forgive your sibling for something that you'd never let a co-worker get away with. God says we have to love our neighbours the same way we love ourselves. The same way we love our parents and our children.

Does that mean you should walk around town handing out money to strangers? Not at all. Keep practicing moderation. Don't take anything to extremes. All you have to do is show the same acceptance toward everyone in your life, not just the few people you're really close to. Give everyone the same level of care that you give yourself.

Another mistake is thinking that you can love your parents or your children more than you love God. I know this is hard for a lot of people to agree with. But think of it this way: when you are enlightened, your attention is focused on God. Why would starting a family change that? In fact, if you let your family steal your focus away from God, you will find that life punishes you in so many ways. It isn't good for you to love your children or your spouse with an overpowering, animal-instinct love that pushes everything aside. True love allows you to remain enlightened and focused on God. It lets you see all your responsibilities and opportunities without being blinded by them. If you let your emotions confuse and blind you—I want to do this, I don't want to do that, I'd do anything for my children—then you end up trapped by sin. Never put your mistaken ideas about your family's best interests ahead of God's laws.

True love is like nothing else in life, but you can't experience it while you're holding on to your sins. As long as you're driven by the tiniest amount of sin, the love you experience will be warm and fuzzy sometimes, but it won't be pure acceptance.

Let's take our understanding of love even further. The Bible tells you to love your neighbour as you love yourself, but it also tells you to love your enemies. When I've been hurt by people in the past—or rather, when people have tried to hurt me—I have always taken an analytical approach. I would study the situation from every angle and try to understand why they wanted to hurt me. And do you know what? I always came back to this deep conviction that it all came from a higher power. Either the painful situation was a punishment that I had done something to deserve, or it was an opportunity that was supposed to help me grow. Love was what helped me accept trouble calmly, without getting worked up about it. When someone stole my laptop, I thought to myself, "That's interesting. I wonder what I can learn from this?" Love gives you this incredible ability to look at everything that happens to you from a positive point of view. Instead of immediately assuming the worst about a person who tries to cause me pain, I keep my mind curious and open. It's a thousand times better to be naive, sincere, and kind than to be suspicious and cynical.

Philosophy

The true essence of love consists in giving up the consciousness of oneself, forgetting oneself in another self, yet in this surrender and oblivion having and possessing oneself alone. —Hegel

This quote is the pinnacle of my philosophy. It distils everything I've been teaching for years. I've always told people that if you want to live by your heart, you have to tell your ego to take a hike. You have to live like your 'I' doesn't even exist. There's no such thing as 'I want' or 'I don't want.' You have to erase all of that. Let go of your plans and preferences and just trust in God. Nobody likes this advice. It's hard to see how losing yourself means that you actually belong to yourself. But that's how it works.

When I was younger, I used to get attached to the physical circumstances of my life and to the friends and family I saw every day. But when I moved away from home, all of that dropped away: I had no friends, no family nearby, nothing to distract me anymore. And that's exactly when I became my truest self. My ego went away completely, and I was able to accept life as it came to me. I still live that way.

There are a lot of people who have spent their whole lives stuck in this tiny comfort zone, like a prison they designed for themselves. And the pandemic was the first time they were forced to get out of that comfort zone. It's a scary thing to find out that you can't function without your comfort zone. Without being on autopilot. You realise just how weak you are. Strength is when you understand that you aren't in charge. You can't dictate how your life goes. Nothing you 'own' really belongs to you. If I lose everything I have tomorrow, it won't affect my spiritual state in the least. You won't see me screaming and crying and shaking my fist at the sky. Why? Because I know that, in reality, I don't 'have' anything to lose. With God above me, all the things that surround me—my body, the place where I live, the material things that you would consider mine—are just props.

Once you have that deep understanding of the unimportance of the physical facts of your life, you stop feeling so angry at people. Your fear and resentment melt away. That's the whole secret. That's what Hegel was talking about.

Questions and Answers about Love

Question: How am I supposed to love someone without becoming attached to them?

Attachment and love are two very different things. You can be attached to someone because of greed, fear, or even pride, but you get confused and call it love. When you are attached to someone and depend on them for your happiness, that isn't love. Relationships built on sinful attachments fail over time because that true love and acceptance isn't there. A couple starts to fight about who spends the most time with their friends or whose parents they're going to spend the holidays with. Once they have kids, they fight about who gets more time to themselves and who does more of the childcare. They fight about the family budget: if you made that big purchase for your hobby, why can't I buy this thing for mine?

You know what I find interesting? That possessiveness is what people call love, when it's really just attachment and dependence. Attachment causes people to stay in terrible relationships where both partners are grinding each other down and preventing each other from living healthy lives. They're afraid they won't find anyone better. They're afraid of being alone. They feel like their partner actually *belongs* to them. Maybe they stand to gain financially from staying with their partner. There are lots of bad reasons people get together and stay together. Love is something else entirely.

This doesn't just apply to intimate relationships. You can say you love your job or your city or your church, but if you're dependent on a feeling you get from that connection, then it isn't love. It's an animal instinct. Love is the opposite: a soft, wise feeling of acceptance.

Question: You say that if I follow the seven virtues, I'll be able to accept everything around me the way it is, but how am I supposed to react when someone does something wrong? Am I supposed to pretend like they did the right thing?

Let me remind you that no one is all good or all bad. We're like empty bottles that can be filled with good or bad contents. Today, I've got two sins turned on at five per cent each, three virtues turned on at twenty per cent each, and the rest of my virtues are all turned off. Everybody else live the same way: some days you're more driven by virtue, other days you're more driven by sin. So, when you see someone do wrong, you don't need to judge the bottle. And you don't need to judge the contents, either. If a person is doing wrong, you can avoid them so you aren't influenced by them, but you don't need to point a finger and say, "What they're doing is wrong!"

Question: Do you think that I shouldn't be in a relationship until I get a handle on my sins and turn on my virtues?

I don't know if you can be in a relationship or not. I'm just showing you how the system works. That's where I bring value. I'm like a hacker who has the source code for life, and it's my life's work to share it with you in my books and classes. All of my content comes with a big caveat, however: my lessons are places where you can tinker with the algorithm called life, taking it apart, looking at how it works. But that doesn't mean you should jump up and start making radical changes in your own personal life. If you walk around labelling your every action as sinful or virtuous, you've missed the point. Except when you're reading this book or listening to one of my classes, I don't want you to think about sin and virtue at all. Growing as a person and strengthening your virtues is not like studying for a test. It's more like building a house. While you read my book, you're working through the process of building your new life. When you set it down, it's time to actually live in the house you built.

If you let your analytical mind have free rein and ask yourself questions like, "Am I virtuous enough to be in a long-term relationship?" or "Which of my family members is the most sinful?" then you will never be happy. You'll just run around pointing fingers and labelling you and your loved ones' actions. That's no better than being a robot.

What I want for you is the opposite of that kind of robotic analysis. I want you to cleanse your mind, calm it, and set it free. How can you do that? By reading what I can tell you about the source code to life and then—this is key—letting it go. Once you know how the world works, don't ruminate and worry about whether you're doing the right thing.

Think about all the millions of people going about their regular lives right this very minute. Imagine a young woman stopping for a lemonade at a sidewalk cafe. Then image a young man walking by on the sidewalk and smiling at her.

Neither of them is considering whether they're actions are sinful or virtuous. They're just living.

I can spend a month or more talking with a close friend about important life questions as I'm doing in this book. But when we're done, we put it away and go back to living our lives and doing the things friends do together.

Just live your life. Do what you want to do. That includes going out with people and making long-term commitments. You'll notice that the things you want to do are a little different after you do the work of reading through this whole book. The simple act of reading this book will help you brainstorm new ways of living. And when you're done, you can just let go of your expectations and see how your life becomes brighter, with more opportunities and stronger friendships.

So, should you avoid romantic commitments until you feel like you've made progress in your growth? Again, I don't know. But if you feel drawn to a person, why not see where it takes you? Getting to know someone isn't the same as promising to marry them. Try to live lightly and let developments lead you instead of labelling and controlling everything. That's a much wiser way to live, and it's also the way of moderation.

Question: If all people are sinful, does that mean it's impossible for a human being to know true love?

It's entirely possible that some of you have experienced true love. If you set my books down and go outside feeling euphoric, like you're on a better wavelength than you've ever known before, and you run into someone who is also being driven by virtue at that moment, then you might find yourselves talking to each other like nothing around you exists. I'm sure that's happened to some of you. Coincidences happen, where just when you've turned on your seven virtues, you encounter another person who is also powered by virtues and you hit it off. In that moment, that's true love. It probably didn't last, did it? A day goes by, and then another day. It's hard for you to support each other in that euphoria. Both of you have jobs and other friends. First one of you and then the other lost that focus when your sins switched back on.

The same thing has happened to me many times. I would feel something wonderful switch on inside me—my inner fire—and then I'd lose it. Afterwards, I'd walk around for days wondering what happened. What did I do wrong?

So, I started to observe and take notes on which people and situations turned on my inner fire and which ones put it out. Love is the same way. You can find this magical true love with someone and then watch it disappear like the morning fog.

Here's where it gets difficult, though. You can observe yourself and start to understand what actions you take that turn on your sin, but you can't control the person you love and force them to look for those insights in their own life. All you can do is try to keep your own fire alight and wait to see what happens with them.

Question: If I learn to accept everything and love everyone, you say I'll be happy. But won't that make me not want to grow any more or do anything to make the world a better place?

There's more to it than that. Imagine a person who is driven by sin: they're at work, walking down the street, or surfing the web. And whatever they're doing, they feel annoyed, angry, and envious. They feel like they have to compete with the people around them. No matter what they do, they can't quite measure up. Now imagine a person who is powered by virtue. Outwardly, they're doing pretty much the same things: they're sitting at work, or walking down the street, or surfing the web. The difference is that they feel peaceful and happy. And when they walk down the street or surf the web, the virtuous person notices that certain things catch their attention, and they follow those things. If someone grabs your attention and you feel drawn to them, you go along with it.

So, on the one hand, a virtuous person who loves and accepts everything and everyone doesn't need to work hard to prove themselves. But that doesn't mean they aren't motivated. When you live by virtue, the force that moves you is a strong one, but it works differently. You don't struggle and strive all the time because you're angry and you want more money and things or because you want to be in another place with other people. You put in plenty of effort—at work, at home, exercising, eating right—not because of pride or greed, but because you enjoy the process. Some higher power tells you what to do, and you're glad to do it.

When you live by your mind and follow the rules of the world, your thoughts and desires don't really belong to you. You end up working hard to achieve things that don't feed your soul, copying others instead of becoming your true self. That's what most people call 'ambition.'

What I hear in your question is that you're worried that virtue will make you lazy. You're worried that you will lose your ambition if you follow my instructions for changing your life. But that couldn't be farther from the truth. Your ambitions will change, but they will come to reflect your deepest, truest self.

Question: Are you saying I can have true love for more than one person?

The true, philosophical love that comes from virtue is neutral. When you accept people for who they are, you don't limit that acceptance to a small handful of your closest friends.

But if you're asking about romantic love, that's a little different. I'm not suggesting that you go out and practice polyamory. Find a person who fuels your inner fire and try to do the same for them. And if it doesn't work out, remember that there are plenty of good people out there. Sometimes, we miss our chances with people. There are plenty of backups. I've been someone's backup before, and I'm sure it will happen again. Here's the thing: if you let virtue lead you, then all the romantic partners who come your way will be good, loving people. Like attracts like.

The same thing happens to sinful people: they always attract the wrong romantic partners. It's like you're stuck on a merry-go-round of people with different names and faces, but all of them make you upset or angry the exact same way.

Do you see the hope in this? It means that when you change yourself, you change the people who come into your life. It's a powerful force.

♥

A Final Word

In this half of the book, we looked at the seven virtues that make up the human heart and learned how certain actions can reinforce those virtues and strengthen your connection with the higher power. I showed you how choosing a life of virtue will give you joy, free you from fear, and provide your life with meaning. You will have faith in yourself and be able to choose what is right and what is wrong *for you*.

Reader, I'm grateful for whatever put my book in your hands. I hope you managed to read it all the way through, and I hope it opened your eyes so you can see life differently now. If this book helped you, write to mail@akinformation.com and let me know. Getting messages from readers is what always energizes me to write the next book!

Next time you feel down on yourself, don't give up. Keep living by the rules I've shown you here. Surround yourself with good, kind people. Tend your inner fire. I promise you, it's worth it. Good luck!

Alexandr Korol

Social networks:

Website: https://akinformation.com/
E-mail: mail@akinformation.com
YouTube: https://youtube.com/c/Akinformation
Instagram: https://www.instagram.com/akinformation/
Facebook: https://www.facebook.com/akinformation/